FEAR NEWARK BAY WILL LOSE GOVERNMENT HARBOR FUNDS.

Interest in the several cities on Newark Bay are making energetic efforts to assure the continuance of Government work on Newark Bay by providing for the disposition of the dredging from the bay channel. A committee from the Bayonne Chamber of Commerce has brought the matter before the Board of Commissioners for immediate action.

Secretary William P. Drew informed the commissioners that the Chamber of Commerce has authoritative information that not only will the dredging be stopped but that the money that was appropriated for this purpose will be diverted to some other section of the country. This will mean that the proposed new development that was to have added 400 acres of taxable land, or about 50 city blocks, will be abandoned.

SOME OF THE ADRIATIC'S CREW INSISTED ON A BONUS.

Seventy-eight members of the crew of the White Star liner Adriatic were fined £2 each in the Liverpool courts July 22 by a magistrate after conviction on the charges of conspiring to impede the ship's voyage before leaving New York by walking out, and demanding a bonus.

The firemen and trimmers of the Adriatic demanded a bonus before leaving New York on the latest trip of the vessel because, they declared, they would be compelled to work extra hours in consequence of the desertions of twenty-one firemen. Captain Beadnell was forced to sign an agreement giving the men a bonus of £5 each before they would consent to work the vessel across. The Adriatic left her pier thirty minutes after scheduled time.

GENERAL ITEMS.

THE Independent Coal Corporation, 25 Broadway, New York, announce their appointment to represent at this port the well known firm of John S. Darrell & Co. in connection with the sale of bunker coal to steamers at Bermuda.

THE Panama Canal reports a change in charges for pumping cargoes from ships to storage tanks between the hours of 11 p. m. and 7 a. m. from 6 cents per barrel to ten dollars per hour.

STEAMER Muskogee, to the Humble Oil & Refining Company was placed in berth at Texas City at 9 a. m. July 13 and left at 3 p. m. the same day for New York, after taking in a full cargo of oil.

T. J. KEHOE, general representative for the Admiral-Oriental Line in New York, announced the receipt of a telegram from headquarters of the company in Seattle saying that the steamship President Jefferson had arrived from the Orient with a cargo valued at $13,000,000, of which $6,000,000 was in silk and the remainder in miscellaneous commodities. The liner brought in 390 passengers.

CLEMINGTON Carson, an officer on the training ship Illinois, noted oarsman, sailed for London on the President Van Buren of the United States Lines July 18, where he will go in training preparatory to an attempt to row across the English Channel. Carson is well known for his ability to pull an ordinary row boat through strong currents. His record includes a trip from Albany to the Battery in a rowboat and one around Manhattan Island.

THE French Courts have handed down a decision in the case of the Ocean Steamship Company of Savannah vs the French Ministry of Marine in the sinking of the steamer City of Athens on April 30, 1918 by the French Cruiser Gloria. The decision says that it must be considered an ordinary war loss.

THE following were recently admitted to membership of the Maritime Association of Port of New York: Messrs. John F. Cahalane with Simpson, Spence & Young; G. Christensen with J. W. Cunningham & Co., Inc; Geo. B. Drake, the Texas Company, and Albert Steffgen.

THE British tug Lucienne, from Rotterdam for Vancouver, B. C., passed through Panama Canal on June 20. The tug is 80 feet long 19.8 feet beam and has a speed of 9½ knots on 2 tons of coal daily. The distance from Rotterdam to Vancouver is 9000 nautical miles and she covered half the distance without mishap. She carries a crew of 8 all told. The tolls on her passage through the Canal amounted to $30.75.

CASUALTIES.

Advance (s s), before rrported wrecked at Halifax, NS. Halifax, NS, July 20—The wreck of the str Advance was found to be on fire to-day and was burned to the water's edge. Owners of the wreck are under the impression that the fire was incendiary. About all the cargo had been removed. (✠ July 11.)

Aledo (s s), from Montreal via Helsingfors, arrived at Kalmar July 24 with part of cargo damaged by sea water; steam pipe leaky.

Andania (Br s s), at London, July 3, from Montreal, damaged propeller, supposed by striking submerged wreckage, while approaching the English Channel.

Asia (Dan motor), from Newcastle, N S W, dragged anchors in a heavy gale at Valparaiso July 8 and collided with stmrs Taltol (Chil) and Llamquihue (Chil); damage not known.

Augusta (s s) from Boston for New York grounded in Boston harbor but floated and proceeded to New York and was placed in dry dock there July 20 for examination and repairs.

Basford (tug) recently purchased by the Colorado and Santa Fe Railroad for car-ferry service at Oakland, damaged her propeller when leaving Sabine. She arrived at Galveston July 13 and placed in dry dock for repairs.

Chas L O'Connor (s s), from Portland July 20 for Norfolk put back to former port 21st with engine trouble.

City of Birmingham (Br s s), from Shanghai, etc., for Boston and New York, before reported grounded at Zamboanga June 4, was surveyed June 11 at Singapore, by divers who reported a plate abreast hatch No. 1 on port side was slightly indented. No other damage apparent, and she was allowed to proceed. (Arrived Port Said July 15.) ✠ June 27.

Colusa (s s)—London, July 18—Stmr Colusa from Tacoma, etc, for Antofagasta, etc, is expected to arrive at Panama tomorrow; cylinder damaged.

Conqueror (bk)—San Francisco, July 18—Bark Conqueror, from San Pedro June 9 for Puget Sound, now out 39 days and not reported; some anxiety felt for safety of vessel.

Constantinople (Br s s), from Constantinople July 8 for New York was aground for twenty four hours on a sand bank in the upper Bosporus. She floated early in the morning of July 6 with the assistance of tugs. Divers' examination showed no damage and she was allowed to proceed.

Deul (s s), from Hamburg July 21 for Montreal, general cargo, had fire in cross bunker in the River Elbe. She was towed back to Hamburg by three tugs; the fire was extinguished; vessel damaged, but cargo thought to be undamaged.

Devolente (s s)—San Francisco, July 18—Tank str Devolente, trading coastwise, grounded near Benicia last night while proceeding up the Sacramento River; vessel in no danger.

Stmr Deuel (s s) from left Hamburg July 21 for Montreal and returned to Hamburg July 23 with coal bunkers on fire.

Diana Dollar (s s) from Manila for Boston and New York, put into Gibraltar June 21 with one propeller blade broken.

Golaa (Nor s s)—Charleston, July 20—Stmr Golaa, from Phila for Tampico, touched bottom on Frying Pan Shoals and put in here; probably for repairs and proceeded later.

Harry Farnum (s s), which left Mobile July 19, anchored below the city with steering gear defective; repairs were made and she proceeded later in the day.

Isonomia (Pan s s), from Newcastle N S W June 10 for San Francisco, was surveyed May 31 at the former port to find out damage caused by floating timber at Tacoma Feb 11. Three propeller blades were found to be bent and some rivets loose in upper arm and outer frame of rudder and in the forepeak. (Arriced San Francisco July 21.)

June (tug)—Beaufort, N C, July 23—Tug Juno (owned by Captain L D Potter, of Wilmington, N C) stranded on Beaufort bar and will probably become a total loss. The chief engineer was lost.

Katahdin, from New York for Tampa and Mobile, put into Charleston July 17 to adjust machinery.

Meanticut (s s)—London, July 20—Stmr Meanticut, Mobile via Havre for Antwerp, went ashore near Dungeness, but floated later. (Arrived Antwerp July 21.)

Newtown (Br s s) from Nassau for Halifax and Montreal before reported ashore inside the Lockport NS light vessel July 3, was floated about July 15, and after receiving temporary repairs proceeded to Halifax where she arrived July 18. She was to be placed on the Marine railway July 19 for survey.

Oregon Pine (schr) from Newcastle N S W, June 17 for Honolulu, while shifting from her berth to moorings at the former port May 28 grounded on a mud bank and remained on for ten hours. She was coal laden.

Oriflamme (Br tank s s), from Southampton July 17 for Sand Key, while at Havre July 9, had slight fire aboard; no damage.

Pipestone County (s s)—London, June 23—Stmr Pipestone County, from Philadelphia and New York via Havre for Dunkirk, was in collision July 23 off Calais with str Amiral Jaureguiberry. Both vessels proceeded to Dunkirk.

President (propeller) engaged in transferring mails in New York had machinery trouble in the bay July 23 and was towed to her berth.

Ruth Martin (schr) Boston, July 23—Damage estimated at over $5,000 resulted from fire on board schr Ruth Martin at East Boston this afternoon. The blaze started in cabin, burning through roof and spreading to mainsail and rigging. Fire quickly extinguished by fire department. Cause of fire not definitely known, thought to have been caused by a blow torch used by workmen repairing. She was owned by John J. Martin but recently sold to Woodstock Lumber Company, reported for about $10,000.

Scatwell (Br s s), from Montreal, arrived at Glasgow July 23, damaged.

Singapore (Br s s) from Calcutta for Buenos Ayres, before reported at Lourenco Marques with fire and stranding damages. Completed repairs July 7 and could proceed with 1700 tons of gunmer, soda and other sound cargo aboard. A quantity of cargo was damaged by fire on ship and some later on wharf. (✠ July 4).

Songdal, (Nor s s)—Stmr Songdal, lying in dry dock, at New York July 20 had a fire among waste in engine room; damage slight; two men slightly burned. (Left New York July 22 for Montreal.)

Tongking (Dan motor), London, July 20—Wireless to Barbados from motor Tongking, from Antwerp, etc for San Pedro, San Francisco, etc., states vessel has slight fire in No 2 hold, in lat 15 N, lon 70 W; vessel steering north; has 74 pass aboard. (Arrived Colon about July 23)

Weert (Ger schr)—Schr Weert from Mobile for Port Spain, put into Macoris July 19 damaged.

West Islip (s s), had a slight fire while at San Francisco, July 12. (Not stmr West Inskip, as previously reported.)

Yonan Maru (Jap s s)——Portland, Ore, July 18—Stmr Yonan Maru, with a cargo of lumber and wheat, was refloated from Peacock Spit, at the mouth of the Columbia River, this afternoon, where it went ashore six days ago. The vessel was taken to Astoria for survey. Much of the cargo had been lightered. (✠ July 18.)

The Dominca schooners Carolina, 91 tons, Rich; Higumota, 77 tons, Gomez and Trinidad Sanchez, 70 tons, De Jesus are trading between Santo Domingo and Porto Rico ports.

Valparaiso, July 9—Owing to a heavy gale yesterday La Primera (? Chilean stmr Coquimbo ex La Primera) dragged ashore and was totally wrecked. Danish motor Aria, Taltol (Chil) and Llanquihue (Chil) dragged and collided; extent of damage not yet known. A number of tugs and small craft were wrecked or damaged.—(Lloyd's List.)

The customs and lighthouse tender Kestrel, of the Dominican Government, which arrived at St. Thomas May 13 for repairs left there on July 7 on her return to her station at San Domingo City. She was repaired at a cost of $6,000.

OVERDUE.

Centaurus (Dan sc), from Buffet Harbor about Feb 7 for Oporto.

Escanbie (Ital bk) from Pensacola Dec 18 for Cagliari.

DANGERS TO NAVIGATION.

Reported by the U. S. Hydrographic Office.

July 15—Lat 25 2, lon 87 49, passed a partly submerged spar, which was continuously emerging about two feet and submerging; it was covered with seaweed and apparently attached to submerged wreckage—Stmr. Yoro.

June 24—Lat 41 47, lon 55 45, passed a derelict bottom up and painted red—Hellig Olav, Dan, Peronard; Officer Ericksen.

July 4—Lat 49 46, lon 11 20, passed an upright spar, apparently attached to submerged wreckage—Stmr. Inverarder.

July 12—Lat 28 44, lon 91 11, passed a large tree trunk about 30 feet long and about 4 feet in diameter—Stmr Alabama.

July 2—Lat 42 45, lon 39 05, passed a log about 30 feet long and 1½ feet in diameter—Stmr. President Garfield.

July 6—Lat 33 15, lon 76 50, passed a spar, projecting about 3 feet of wated, apparently attached to submerged wreckage—Stmr Vistula.

July 8—Lat 32 59, lon 78 19, passed a piece of wreckage awash, about 12 feet long and 8 feet wide—Stmr W W Mills.

July 10—About 3 miles 121 degrees from American Shoal Lighthouse, Florida Reefs, sighted a spar, projecting 3 feet out of water, apparently attached to submerged wreckage—Stmr W W Mills.

July 20, lat 19 48, lon 74 06, piece of wreckage floating low in the water—Agwibay; July 20, lat 19, lon 74 33, log 30 feet long, ½ feet in diameter, covered with barnacles—Stmr Steel Exporter.

July 13—Lat 44 2, lon 67 35, passed three logs about 18 feet long and 18 inches in diameter.

July 14—Lat 39 10, lon 67 56, passed a can buoy apparently in good condition—Stmr Ossa.

July 14—Lat 38 9, lon 74 30, passed a conical buoy painted in black and white vertical stripes—Stmr Princeton.

July 5—Lat 24 24, lon 82 28, passed wreckage awash, about 50 feet long by 30 feet wide, apparently the side of a wooden vessel—Stmr Gulf of Mexico.

June 12—Lat 42 3, lon 49, passed three spars, about 30 feet long, lashed together—Stmr Galtymore.

The Canadian Signal Service, Supt H S McGreevy, reports ice sighted as follows:

July 12—Melita, Br, reports lat 48 55, lon 45 12; lat 48 33, lon 47 9; lat 48 15, lon 48 14, and lat 48 7, lon 47 55, sighted bergs.

Turcoman, Br, reports July 1, lat 48 59, lon 46 29, sighted a berg; lat 48 55, lon 46 48, a growler; lat 48 44, lon 47 20, a large berg.

Wearpool, Br, reports July 10, lat 48 30, lon 47 10, sighted a small berg, and lat 48 13 lon 48 3, a large berg.

Cairnross, Br, reports July 16,. lat 48 25, lon 49 20, sighted a berg; lat 48 12, lon 49 45, a large berg, and lat 48 10, lon 49 35, a berg.

Empress of France, Br, reports July 16, lat 51 47, lon 54 46, large bergs; lat 52 03, lon 54 48, a large berg; from Belle Isle to Cape Norman, fifty bergs and growlers; from Cape Norman to Point Amour fifty-one bergs and growlerr; from Point Amour to Greenly Island, ten bergs and growlers; twelve bergs along North Shore; one berg on the track eastward of Flat Island, and one berg and a growler southward of track eastward of St Mary's.

Manchester Hero, Br, July 16, reports first bergs sighted 70 miles eastward of Belle Isle, thence to Point Amour bergs and growlers too numerous to mention.

Point Amour—July 17, thirteen bergs July 12, sixteen bergs.

Belle Isle—July 16, forty bergs and many growlers.

Stmr Alexandra (Dan) reports July 17 sighted iceberg in lat 53 06, lon 52 18; also in lat 52 10, lon 54 30; thence through the Straits to Greenly Island passed numerous bergs and growlers (about 50 pieces); one berg in lat 50 40, lon 58 12.

OCEAN CHARTERS.

The charters of steam and sail vessels reported by Cornish & Co. of New York for the week ended July 21 were as follows:

GRAIN.

Fr stmr Malgache, 2362 tons, Montreal to west Italy, 17c, early Aug.

Br stmr Sheaf Mount, 3207 tons, Montreal to the U K, 2/9, early Aug.

Dan stmr Jelling, 1172 tons, Montreal to Limerick, 3/6, prompt.

Ital stmr Marte, 3295 tons, Montreal to west Italy, basis 16½c, Aug.

PETROLEUM.

Am (tank) stmr Samuel L Fuller, 5072 tons, Tampico to New York, crude, 41c per bbl, option Curacao loading, 42c, July.

Am (tank) stmr Camden, 4153 tons, Los Angeles to a Gulf port, crude, 80c per bbl, Aug.

Nor (tank) stmr Sjomand, 1556 tons, Phila to Germany, products, 32/6, prompt.

Br (tank) stmr Blomfield, 2722 tons, Gulf to Rouen, products, 35/, July.

Am (tank) stmr Lio, 4398 tons, Los Angeles to North of Hatteras, gasoline, 95c per bbl, Sept.

Am (tank) stmr Cassimir, 3030 tons, Tampico to North of Hatteras, ten trips, crude, 35c per bbl, option U S Gulf loading, prompt.

MISCELLANEOUS.

Am stmr Arcturus, 3816 tons, Atlantic range to west Italy, coal, $3, prompt.

Fr stmr Albi, 2503 tons, Atlantic range to Algiers, coal, $2.75, prompt.

Br stmr Caldy Light, 2481 tons, Pensacola to Bristol Channel, pitch, 15/3, Aug.

Ital stmr Ansaldo VII, 3145 tons, Baltimore to the Antwerp - Rotterdam range, coal, $2.10, prompt.

Am stmr Agwistar, 2921 tons, Intercoastal trade, one round trip, at or about $1.35, July.

Ital stmr Lanuvium, 2856 tons, Atlantic range to Savona, coal, at or about $3.10, July.

Am stmr Montpelier, 2813 tons, Intercoastal trade, one trip, at or about $1.50, delivery North of Hatteras, July.

Nor stmr Hallgyn, 4164 tons, Atlantic range to the Continent, coal, $2.10, July.

SOUTH AMERICA.

Br stmr Patrick, 2692 tons, Atlantic range to La Plata, coal, $3.50, prompt.

Nor stmr Cederic, 3080 tons, U S and W C South America trade, one round trip, 92½c, prompt.

Br stmr St Dustan, 3567 tons, Hampton Roads to Rio Janeiro, coal, at or about $3.50, prompt.

DEALS AND TIMBER.

Br stmr Lady Brenda, 1900 tons (previously), Newfoundland to west coast U K, pit props, 42/6, prompt.

Stmr ——, 1000 stds, Miramichi to west Britain or east Ireland, deals, 60/, prompt.

WEST INDIES, ETC.

Dan stmr Svanhild, 1287 tons, West India trade, one round trip, at or about $1.25, prompt.

Dan stmr Nordstjeren, 1338 tons, one or two ports N S Cuba to North of Hatteras, sugar, 12½c, prompt.

Nor stmr Sydfold, 1430 tons, West India trade, one round trip, $1.15, prompt.

PROVINCIAL.

Dan stmr Knud, 2409 tons, Hampton Roads to Montreal, coal, $1, prompt.

Ital stmr San Giuseppe, 2948 tons (previously), Baltimore to Three Rivers coal, about $1.25, prompt.

Dan stmr Sigvald, 719 tons, Gulf to Montreal, lumber, at or about $12, July.

Nor stmr H K Waage, 1166 tons, Miramichi to New York, lumber, p t, Aug.

Br stmr Magdala, 3134 tons, Virginia or Baltimore to Halifax, coal, $1, July-Aug.

Nor stmr Ottawa, 1583 tons, Virginia to Halifax, coal, $1.10, prompt.

Br schr Minas King, 469 tons, New York to St John, NB, coal, $1.25.

Br schr Minas Princess, 465 tons, same.

The British bark *Puritan* was blown ashore on Long Island near Bellport on February 2, 1908. Government Life Savers from the Bellport station used their lifeboat to assist the crew of 16 ashore. The Master and mate remained on board. The vessel was pulled off by wreckers on February 28th. *Photo courtesy of Capt. W.J. Lewis Parker, U.S.C.G.,[Ret.]*

SHIPWRECKS
IN
NEW YORK WATERS

BY

PAUL C. MORRIS & WILLIAM P. QUINN

A Chronology of Ship Disasters from Montauk Point
to Barnegat Inlet from the 1880's to the 1930's

The excursion steamer *Interstate Park* sunk beside her pier in 1924.

Other Books by Paul C. Morris
American Sailing Coasters of the North Atlantic (1973)
Four Masted Schooners of the East Coast (1975)
The Island Steamers (1977) co-author Joseph F. Morin
Schooners and Schooner Barges (1984)
Maritime Sketches (1985)
A Portrait of a Ship (1987)

Other Books by William P. Quinn
Shipwrecks Around Cape Cod (1973)
Shipwrecks Around New England (1978)
Shipwrecks Around Maine (1983)
Shipwrecks Along the Atlantic Coast (1988)

PREFACE

This book is the resultant outgrowth and combination of two large collections of maritime photographs. Bill Quinn met Paul Morris when Bill made a trip to Nantucket Island to do a TV film documentary on the Morris's Ivory Shop. The two men found that they had many interests in common. Both were very much interested in maritime history and both had impressive collections of marine photos. In a very short time they were trading pictures from their collections.

Photography had its birth in the middle of the 19th century and through the years has greatly improved in quality. It is perhaps noteworthy that the development of instant photography, which occurred in the 1880's, was coincidental with the issuing of marine disaster reports from a number of different agencies. Combining these two facts enabled this book.

The collection of the photographs contained in this volume was an effort that continued for over forty five years. The pictures come from a wide and diverse number of sources. Some were donated, a few were purchased and many were copied from files, scrapbooks and private collections. They all portray incidents that occurred fifty or more years ago. Looking at them gives one a chance to go back in time and see into the fate of some of the mariners who trafficked in the waters in and around New York harbor. In most of the photographs shown, it was an unhappy lot.

Shipwrecks were a common happening back in the "good old days". In spite of all of our modern technology, they still happen, although not as frequently as they did fifty or one hundred years ago. Evidence of some of the old shipwrecks still manifest themselves today. Occasionally after a particularly hard northeast storm, the blackened frames of some long forgotten wreck will be exposed on a wind swept beach. There are also still to be found in some backwater ports the remains of vessels unable to carry on and who were left there to rot away in silence with the passing of years.

The waters in and around New York contain their own share of skeletal vessel remains. Kill Van Kull, a stretch of water to the north of Staten Island, was once used as a dumping area for vessels either unwanted or unable to carry on. Tied to aging piers, both ships and wharves were left to decay and sink into the mud on the bottom. The Witte yard on Staten Island holds the remains of many vessels of different types that will in all probability never set to sea again.

While shipwrecks are nothing new, they still hold a strange fascination for most of us. This volume will give the viewer a chance to go back in time and relive some of the pathos and hard times that became the fate of some of those hardy mariners of yesteryear.

This book is dedicated to

our dedicated wives:

Signe Ann Morris

and

Mary R. Quinn

The poggy boat *Falcon* broke her back on a bar and lay sunk in 1906.

CONTENTS

LIST OF PHOTOGRAPHS

A contrast in views of New York was depicted in early paintings of the area. The above view is titled "New York from the heights near Brooklyn in 1823." The painting below is titled "View of New York from Brooklyn Heights in 1849." The change was notable from an idyllic scene to one of hustle and bustle in the harbor, perhaps an omen of times to come. The reproductions were taken from the book "Ships and Shipping of Old New York".

Chapter One

New York, the so-called "Big Apple", has a fascinating and long history; one that has been written about many times. However, as often found within the proverbial "apple", the port has a "wormy side"; a worm that must be labeled "shipwreck". One can only guess at the total number of vessels lost upon entering, leaving or operating within this famous port. To say the least, the numbers are legion.

It was thirty-two years after Columbus discovered America that the first known Europeans dropped anchor in what is now New York harbor. A Florentine navigator in the service of France, in a vessel named the *Dauphine*, arrived in the spring of 1524. His name was Giovanni da Verrazano. More than a few years later he was to have a bridge named in his honor; a bridge that was built over the same area where his trusty little vessel probably rode at anchor.

The next year, following Verrazano, a Portuguese explorer, working for the king of Spain, charted the mouth of what we now call the Hudson River. The sailor's name was Esteban Gomez, and he called the great river the "Rio de San Antonio". Most people have forgotten about poor old Gomez and certainly his name for the river didn't hold fast for any length of time. There were undoubtedly a few other subsequent explorers who poked the bow of their vessel into those new waters. However, it wasn't until after Henry Hudson rounded Sandy Hook on September 3, 1609, and proceeded to sail up the river that now bears his name that Europeans began to think about the commercial possibilities of this particular area.

Hudson was looking for a northern passage to China and although he failed to find what he was in search of, he did sail a considerable distance up the Hudson. While doing this he stopped and traded with the indians bringing aboard the *Half Moon* many beaver and otter skins. Needless to say, the Dutch East India Company, Hudson's employer, was quick to realize the importance of the potential for fur trading possibilities.

Between 1610 and 1612, two Dutchmen, Hendrik Christiaensen and Adriaen Block, visited Manhattan's shores and successfully traded with the indians for furs. After the completion of several voyages from Holland, they again sailed forth sometime during the fall of 1613, in two vessels named *Fortyn* and *Tigre*. Captain Christiaensen sailed the *Fortyn* up the Hudson and founded the first Dutch trading post in America at Fort Nassau. Captain Block, with the *Tigre*, remained behind to spend the winter of 1613-14 trading for furs on Manahattan Island.

His efforts were most successful and by January or February 1614, his vessel was loaded with furs and being made ready for the return voyage to Holland. Unfortunately for Captain Block, the *Tigre* somehow caught fire and burned to the waters edge, making it the first large vessel, one of many, many hundreds to follow, that was to lay its bones on the bottom in or near New York harbor.

Captain Block was not a man easily beaten. He and his crew built log cabins for shelter and the following spring built for themselves a forty- foot vessel which they named *Onrust*. Aboard this little vessel they proceeded to sail up through what we now call "Hell Gate", through Long Island Sound, on to Block Island, which Block named after himself, and finally back to Holland.

More Dutch sailors and settlers were soon to follow. In 1620, a Dutch vessel carrying such a group was cast ashore on Sandy Hook. By the close of the 1620's, the Dutch had built a fort, purchased the island from the Manhattan indians for sixty guilders, named it New Amsterdam and the settlement was soon doing a thriving fur trade with the indians in the surrounding area.

Above: The steamer *Lexington* caught fire on Long Island Sound during the night of January 13, 1840. Captain George Child with a crew of forty, tried desperately to head the vessel toward shore. There were 150 passengers on board and a full cargo of cotton bales. This material fed the flames until the fire was out of control. Later the ship sank and there were only four survivors. Early publications used this type of artwork to illustrate shipwrecks, and, as can be seen, "artist's license" was used here. There were no boats to help the passengers as shown in the lithograph. *Photo reproduction courtesy of the Peabody Museum of Salem.* **Below:** The trauma of shipwreck was periodically depicted in magazines with lithographs. This is the United States steamer *Powhatan* in a storm, with tattered sails and being inundated with huge waves. The sketch was made by G.T. Douglas, U.S.N. and was published in the May 12, 1877 issue of Harpers Weekly.

In the 1660's, the English took over control of New Amsterdam and named it New York in honor of James, Duke of York. During the late 1600's and early 1700's the port grew in size as commerce increased. However, when viewed by the standards that we hold dear today, we would probably be inclined to regard New York's then growing trade as "tainted", to say the least. Part of this growing commerce was based upon the slave trade and visiting pirates soon found the port was a safe haven for the sale of their "goods". Smuggling also became a favored occupation for many who wished to circumvent British duties and taxes.

New Yorkers have always been an independent lot and during the difficult pre-revolutionary war days, they often expressed their displeasure with British rule. Few people realize that New Yorkers had a "tea party" of their own on April 22, 1774, in which they dumped eighteen cases of hated British tea into New York harbor.

During the long struggle for independence from Great Britain, New Yorkers were quick to seize upon the financial advantages that could be derived from privateering and many privately sponsored ships of war were sent out from New York to prey upon British shipping. A large number of these vessels were successful, much to the delight and economic advancement of the sponsors back home.

After the successful conclusion of the Revolutionary War, New Yorkers jumped into the business of deep water trading with new and unbounded enthusiasm. However, England, along with an old ally, France, were soon to become troublesome adversaries. Both countries, while waging war upon one another, stopped and seized our ships and goods. Britain also engaged in the indignant practice of impressing our seamen.

After our winning the War of 1812, and with the end of Napoleonic rule in France, these hated activities were brought to an end. However, during the period of hostilities our merchant fleets suffered greatly, especially from the embargoes that had been instituted by our own government. New York ship owners, as all other American shipping interests, were at a very low ebb following the Treaty of Ghent in December of 1814.

Aside from its unique geographical location, there were two very historic happenings that occurred during the early 1800's that helped put New York "on the map" as one of the greatest seaports in history.

The first was the start of regular packet service to and from New York and England by the famous Black Ball Line in 1818. Prior to this, ships sailed on an irregular basis and usually only when a full cargo manifest had been obtained. Passengers were carried, but cargo was of paramount importance. It took several years of sailing on fixed schedules for the idea to catch the attention of the general public, but once proven, the packet ship service boomed and trade, both in commodities and passengers, blossomed forth much to the advantage of New York.

Secondly, and of as much if not more importance, was the opening of the Erie Canal in 1825. This great feat of engineering allowed passenger and freight service to the newly expanding interior of the northeastern United States. Produce from inland farms and manufactured goods from the east coast and Europe were traded and sold from the barge trips back and forth. From the Great Lakes to the Hudson and thence to New York, the traffic grew steadily and Manhattan shippers and merchants began enlarging their fleets to accommodate the expanding trade.

As shipments increased overseas, they also grew larger along shore. An ever growing coastal fleet, which was protected by Federal law from foreign intervention, was soon crowding our eastern ports. With all of this increase, New York soon became the hub of shipping on the east coast of the United States, outdoing its old rivals; Boston and Salem.

In the twenty years preceding the Civil War, New York shipbuilders were turning out ever faster vessels. The beautiful clippers of the late 1840's and early 1850's set records that would forever make wooden American sailing ships the champions of the seas and the envy of the world.

People from in and around New York began early in the 1800's to experiment with the building of steamboats. Robert Fulton's successful operation of his steamboat *Clermont* on the Hudson River, between Albany and New York, in 1807, marked the beginning of coastal travel by steamboat. Others were soon to follow.

On March 21, 1815, a Nantucketer by the name of Captain Elihu S. Bunker, took his 134 foot, sloop rigged steamboat *Fulton,* through Hell Gate and delivered his passengers at New Haven, Connecticut. This was a "first" for steam power through that noted, dangerous stretch of water in the East River. By the time that the Civil War had broken out in 1860, coastal steamboats

Above: The steamer *Stonington,* while running in dense fog, rammed into the steamer *Narragansett* in Long Island Sound on June 11, 1880. The accident resulted in the loss of fifty lives. The *Narragansett* caught fire and burned. This illustration is from a collection of Currier & Ives prints, which were very popular in the late nineteenth century. *Photo reproduction courtesy of the Peabody Museum of Salem.* **Below:** Early on the morning of March 14, 1886, an unknown three masted schooner ran into the Cunard liner *Oregon* about fifteen miles south of Moriches, Long Island. Historians believe that the schooner was the *Charles H. Morse* as she was carrying a cargo of coal and disappeared the same time. The collision stove a huge hole in the side of the steamer. About eight hours later she sank to the bottom with only her masts showing above water. The 896 passengers and crew were transferred to the German steamer *Fulda* and brought to New York the next day. The steamer was a total loss. *Photo courtesy of Hank Keatts*

were giving the passenger carrying sailing vessels a "run for their money".

Prior to the Civil War, if one wished to travel north or south, the easiest and most comfortable way was to go by water. Road travel over unpaved, muddy and bumpy routes on stage coaches was frequently a hazard to one's health. Travel by sea was by far the more relaxing and often the quicker way to move about. However, it was by no means absolutely secure or safe. Vessels of all types, both large and small, could be seen in great numbers scurrying along our coastline and entering our large ports. The every day seascape as one viewed it in the mid 1800's, was one filled with action, adventure and vitality. However, with all of this water bourne travel, danger often lurked around the next headland, or after the next sunset.

Navigation then was most primitive when compared to today's methods. Weather forecasting was more often dependent on "Cap'n Josh's game leg", than on any scientific approaches. Over the years, with thousands of vessels making their way to and from the port of New York, it's small wonder that there were shipwrecks, collisions, fires, freeze-ups, sinkings and other tragedies that befell the mariner and his trusting passengers. As we look back in time we can only wonder at the enormity of the mishaps.

On March 30, 1889, the steamship *City of Savannah* ran into the three masted schooner *Lester A. Lewis* off Sandy Hook Lightship in a snowstorm. Forty-six year old Captain Hatch of the schooner was killed when the steamer cut through his cabin and sheered off the entire port stern quarter of the vessel. The schooner stayed afloat on her cargo of lumber. She was later placed in a dry-dock and repaired. *Photo courtesy of the Mariners Museum, Newport News, Virginia.*

Above: The British bark *Winderemere* was in stays and drifted ashore during a snowstorm and northeast gale at Deal Beach, north of Asbury Park, New Jersey on March 18, 1892. The Life Savers from the Deal station removed the crew of forty-eight men and the storm moved the vessel higher up on the beach. The 3,275 ton, square rigged London vessel was only a few months old. She was re-floated on March 29th by the Merritt Wrecking Company and towed to Staten Island. *Photo courtesy of the Mariners Museum, Newport News, Virginia.* **Below:** The German bark *Dr. Seigert* was struck by a line squall on the night of July 22, 1892 and laid over on her beam ends with the masts overhanging the wharf. The crew managed to crawl off the vessel which was brought back on an even keel the next day. The bark suffered some damage in the accident.

The schooner *Lewis King* of Ellsworth, Maine, went ashore in stormy weather at Montauk Point, Long Island on December 18, 1887. The six crewmen and one passenger dropped to the beach from the jibboom and walked to the Life Saving Station at Ditch Plain. Many salvage attempts were made but the hull was a total loss.

Above: On August 12, 1892, The Iron Steamboat steamer *Cepheus* struck a hidden obstruction near Coney Island. She suffered a large hole in her hull. The Captain ran her into shoal water at Norton Point to prevent her from sinking in deep water. The vessel was raised six days later by salvagers from the Chapman Derrick & Wrecking Company and towed to a Brooklyn dock. **Below:**The British brigantine *Highlander* on a voyage from Santa Cruz, Cuba for New York City went aground on Fishers Island on February 13, 1893. She developed a leak at sea and the crewmen were at the pumps constantly to keep her afloat. The Chapman Wrecking Company removed her cargo and the vessel went to pieces on the beach.

The British schooner *Valkyrie* went ashore on the south side of Stepping Stones Lighthouse on February 19, 1893. The vessel had been at anchor off City Island in a northwest gale and was blown aground with her anchors dragging. The schooner was pulled off on February 21st after her cargo of coal had been removed. She was posted missing with all hands in September, 1893.

Above: On March 25, 1893, the German oil tanker *Gluckauf* was lost in the fog. She went ashore on Fire Island beach opposite Sayville, Long Island. The vessel was hard on the beach when wreckers boarded her. She was later abandoned and was a total loss. This ship was the prototype of today's giant oil tankers, the first of her kind with the engines aft and tanks forward. The tanker was equipped with square sails on her foremast and fore and aft sails on the other two masts. This photograph was taken about two years after her wreck and the hull had become a tourist attraction. The name on her bow, *Gluckauf,* in big brass letters a foot tall, meant "good luck" or "lucky one", the irony of fate. *Photo courtesy of the Suffolk Marine Museum, West Sayville, New York.* **Below:** The fishing schooner *Mary F. Kelly* was anchored off Manasquan Beach, New Jersey on the night of August 24, 1893, when a violent storm bore down on her, snapping her anchor cable and driving her ashore. When the schooner hit the outer bar, a huge wave swept over her deck carrying three men, including the Captain, to their deaths. Seven men were rescued by the Life Savers but another man was found dead in the cabin when the seas abated. *Photo courtesy of the Mariners Museum, Newport News, Virginia.*

Above: The coal barge *Milton* in tow of the tug *Scandinavian* ran aground near Astoria, Long Island on November 23, 1893. The vessel was carrying a cargo of 1,400 tons of coal. She lay with half her length hanging over a bar in ninety feet of water. The Chapman Wrecking Company salvaged the cargo but the vessel was a total loss. **Below:** The New York pilot boat *Joseph F. Loubat* went ashore at Amagansett on Long Island in foggy weather on January 16, 1894. Life Savers removed the crew and tried to refloat the vessel but without success. The schooner was later pulled off the beach in a damaged condition. She is shown hauled out in a dry-dock in New York, for repairs.

Above: The French steamship *La Champagne* while proceeding slowly in dense fog ran aground just below Fort Hamilton on May 6, 1894. The ship had cut her speed to four knots as pilot James J. Keely threaded his way through the narrows. The 329 passengers were taken off by the transfer boat *Rosa*. The Merritt Derrick & Wrecking Company removed several hundred tons of cargo into lighters and the ship was refloated the next day. **Below:** On July 17, 1894, the bark *Emma T. Crowell* was consumed by fire when her cargo of 39,332 cases of petroleum burned the vessel to the water's edge. The accident occurred about twelve miles south of Fire Island at 6:20 in the evening while the ship was enroute to Shanghai. The entire crew was picked up by the British steamer *Runic* and transferred to the Sandy Hook Lightship. The burned out hull was towed to the Erie Basin breakwater by the Chapman steamer *Hustler*. Some of the cargo in the lower holds was salvaged.

Above: A fire of unknown origin gutted the full-rigged ship *Gen. Knox* at pier 19 on the East River on August 18, 1894. Half the cargo of kerosene, resin, creosote and turpentine had been loaded aboard when the ship caught fire. New York City firemen poured water on the blazing vessel, flooding the ship and she sank at the dock. The ship was a total loss but the hull was raised and later was converted to a schooner barge. **Below:** The British ship *Glenesslin* caught fire in the afterhold at 11 p.m. on the night of Sept. 23, 1984. Firefighters filled the hold with water and the ship sank beside the pier at Watson's Stores in Brooklyn. To salvage the vessel, the Chapman Wrecking Company moved in three derricks and the steamer *Hustler*. The wreckers pumped the water out and refloated the *Glenesslin* on Sept. 25th.

Above: The fishing schooner *Maria Louise* was battling gale winds and high seas on October 10, 1894, when her sails were blown away. The captain anchored his vessel off Highland Beach, New Jersey. The wind dragged the vessel ashore and it became a total wreck. The schooner was high enough on the beach for the crew to step ashore where they were met by Life Savers, who took them to the Spermaceti Cove station. **Below:** The schooner *Albert Mason* went ashore on Ellis Island on December 27, 1894 during a storm. The vessel damaged a small building when it was blown ashore. On January 11th the schooner was pulled off with little damage and dry-docked for repairs.

The British schooner *Viola* aground at Matinnecock, Long Island Sound on December 27, 1895. The cargo of 5,000 board feet of lumber was transferred to lighters. The vessel re-floated on January 7, 1896 and towed to New York. A report from the New York Maritime Register states that "The *Viola* is badly chafed and was leaking about 500 strokes per hour." Her crew had to man the pumps continuously to keep her from sinking.

One of the most appalling wrecks on the east coast in 1895 was the stranding of the schooner *Louis V. Place* on Long Island. Gale winds and heavy seas prevailed and the schooner was described as a floating iceberg. The crew had climbed into the rigging to await rescue. The life savers attempted to launch a boat but the seas were too high and the small boat was dashed back on the beach by the huge waves. A line, fired out over the vessel, was not picked up because of the debilitated condition of the men, waiting for rescue and numbed by the cold. On the second day, six men succumbed to exposure before the Life Savers could get a boat out through the high surf to rescue the two survivors left. One survivor, William Stevens said: "Well, it was a rough experience. The masts of the vessel swayed back and forth all day, and every moment I expected would be our last. But I don't seem to feel it much. With a pan of baked beans and a good smoke, I could have held out for a number of hours longer." The other survivor, S.J. Nelson, later died from the ordeal. The schooner, 735 tons, bound from Baltimore to New York City with a cargo of coal was a total loss. *Photo by Anderson, courtesy of the Suffolk Marine Museum, West Sayville, New York.*

Above: The Sound steamer *Continental* ran up on Hog's Back Reef at Ward's Island, near Hell Gate in dense fog just after midnight on March 31, 1895. Her 80 passengers were asleep when the accident occurred. They were all taken off the next morning. The ship was ultimately pulled off the reef and went back into service between New York City and New Haven, Connecticut. **Below:** The schooner *Lester A. Lewis,* bound from Norfolk for New York ran up on Romer Shoal at 9 p.m. on April 20, 1895 and sank. Cause of the accident was an error in navigation. The vessel was refloated the next day and towed to New York in a waterlogged condition by the Chapman Derrick & Wrecking Company. Much of the deck cargo was lost and damage was heavy to the rigging. Her mizzenmast was broken off below deck and the maintopmast was lost.

Above: The *SS Olinda* went on the rocks off Goose Hummock on the south side of Fisher's Island on June 11, 1895, in thick fog. She had on board a Fall River pilot and he ran the vessel too close to shore. Her cargo of cork and empty barrels was saved. A storm broke the vessel in two and the hull remained on the island. **Below:** The steamer *Isabel* ran up on the rocks off Branford, Connecticut on August 4, 1895. This accident caused damage to the vessel but she was pulled off and repaired. She was lost in Long Island Sound when she sank at Shippan Point near Stamford in 1915.

The Fall River Line steamer *Puritan* became lost in dense fog while entering Long Island Sound on November 9, 1895 at three a.m. The ship went up hard and fast on Great Gull Island. The Atlantic Coast Pilot book describes the dangerous area: "The passage between Great Gull Island and Plum Island has a number of known dangers and very irregular bottom with boulders and should be avoided. The part of the passage between Old Silas Rock and Plum Island has been examined by means of a wire drag; boulders with depths of 3 to 10 feet were found." On the next day, two other steamers along with three tugs tried to pull the *Puritan* off the rocks but without success. Salvage men removed the cargo from the grounded steamer and tried again to float her but to no avail. Tugs pulled at her with every tide but she was stuck fast. Divers were sent down to examine the bottom and reported that the rocks did not pierce through the outer skin of the ship. The grounding caused scars and dents on the steel bottom. The problem with the salvage effort was that the front half of the ship was resting on the bottom while the stern half was afloat. A continuing problem was the fact that the *Puritan* went on the rocks at high tide and in order to refloat the ship an equal or higher tide would be needed. Three days after the ship went aground she was pulled off by the efforts of three tugs and ground tackle aboard the steamer. After the ship was pulled off the rocks she was taken to New York and dry-docked for repairs.

    The British steamer *Lamington* came ashore during thick and stormy weather at 7 p.m., on February 4, 1896, two miles east of the Blue Point Life Saving Station on Long Island. The wreck was reported almost immediately to the keeper of the station who notified the Bell Port and Lone Hill stations. The crews from the three stations assembled at the scene and set up the beach apparatus. The vessel was about 400 yards from shore which made operations difficult if not impossible. Four shot lines were fired before one line lay over the steamer. At that time it was almost eleven o'clock at night and the crew of the ship could not find the line. A large fire was built on shore to bolster the spirits of the men aboard the ship. The Life Savers waited all night in stormy weather for daylight. Early the next morning the line was discovered and the apparatus set up. Twenty crewmen were landed and taken to the Blue Point Station where they remained. Tugs were called for and arrived at two o'clock in the afternoon. Wreckers boarded the ship and began preparations to refloat the vessel at the next high tide. The men aboard the ship cast off the life-saving gear and sent a ship's line ashore to maintain communication. During the night of February 5th, the weather grew worse. The wreckers signaled that they wished to be brought ashore. The ship's line parted while it was being hauled off shore and the wind had increased to gale force. The wrecking tugs left to find shelter against the deteriorating weather. The life savers again fired a shot line over the vessel and rigged the breeches buoy. But because of the darkness and high seas it was decided to wait until the daylight hours before attempting a rescue. The vessel was holding fast on the bar and seemed in no danger of breaking up. Life Savers spent another long night on the beach maintaining a large bonfire burning on the beach. At daybreak, the buoy was sent off and nineteen men were landed. The steamer remained stranded and on February 8th, the life savers landed a pony, slung under the breeches buoy. The Life Savers maintained the hawser on the beach for three weeks. In that time they sent off and landed wreckers and crewmen to keep the work of refloating going on until February 26th when the ship was hauled off and towed to New York. The cargo of fruit was lost. The steamer *Lamington* of 1,886 tons, was on a voyage from Gibraltar, Spain to New York City with a crew of 24.

Chapter Two

New York harbor is well suited to the needs of a large port. It is very spacious, with a water frontage covering approximately 771 miles. The lower Bay has an area of around one hundred square miles and from the Narrows, where the Verrazano Bridge is located, up to the Battery at the head of the Upper Bay, One would have to travel over five miles in an area covering seventeen square miles.

There are three major accesses to New York harbor. One is from the Hudson River. Another is from Long Island Sound, through the East River. The major entrance for most large shipping is from the south, by way of the Ambrose Channel. Actually there are several channels leading in from the south and if one wanted to try it, another approach to the Upper Bay could be made by way of the "Kills", around Staten Island which is also a part of New York.

All of these approaches have their navigational problems. Tricky winds, fickle eddies, ice and fog with waiting underlying rocks are hazards to be found on the Hudson. The East River was a notoriously dangerous place and can still cause trouble, particularly at Hell Gate, where the Harlem River, coming down from the Hudson, enters the East River. At this point, unpredictable rips, currents and eddies often threw many vessels on the rocks located on each side of the channel.

One of the most famous of the early losses occurred in 1780, when the British frigate *Hussar,* struck Pot Rock in Hell Gate and foundered while she had American prisoners on board along with a reported fortune that was supposed to be used as pay for British troops. Several people have tried to find and reclaim the treasure aboard but all have failed. Simon Lake, the submarine inventor, tried in 1937 but was unable to locate the wreck with its supposed four million in gold coin.

As traffic increased with the passage of time, the number of losses in Hell Gate grew to a staggering amount. By the 1870's, the costs during some years exceeded two and a half million dollars. Hallett's Point, was a rocky reef seven hundred feet wide which extended three hundred feet into the channel at Hell Gate. It caused rips and currents that ended the career of many a vessel that was trying to thread its way through this troublesome area. This deadly outcropping was finally removed with the aid of 52,000 pounds of explosives in a blast that shook the entire area on September 24, 1876. Navigating Hell Gate thereafter was improved but it still remained a dangerous place due to the difference in tide levels between Long Island Sound and the Upper Bay. The resulting furious currents that roared through the East River often cast an unwary helmsman on the rocks. Tows through this troublesome spot were particularly at risk. Vessel collisions also occurred often at Hell Gate.

The entrance to New York harbor from the south was not without its risks as well. Passing to the north of Sandy Hook, vessels entering or leaving the port could at one time navigate one of three frequently used channels. In 1899, the East Channel was improved and in 1900 was renamed the Ambrose Channel in honor of John Wolf Ambrose, a man who had for many years advocated channel improvement in New York harbor.

Even with channel improvements there were still many traps awaiting those who were unfamiliar or unwary. Romer Shoals, located just to the west of Ambrose Channel, over the years, captured more than its share of passing vessels with an attending loss of life. The shoal received its name from the loss of the pilot schooner *William J. Romer,* which in 1863 struck a submerged wreck at that spot resulting also in the death of one of the pilots on board the schooner.

On February 6, 1896, gale winds and pouring rain hit New York City and raised havoc in the harbor. The ship *J. B. Walker* was being towed from Brooklyn when she was cast ashore on Liberty Island while still being pulled by the tugs. The ship had discharged her cargo and was "flying light" without any ballast. She was to load with case oil for China when the accident occurred. The *J.B. Walker* was successfully refloated by the Chapman Wrecking & Derrick Company.

Dating from its very early history, pilotage was required for foreign vessels traveling the waters leading into or out of New York. In the early 1800's, both New York and New Jersey were sending out pilots to assist in the safe navigation of vessels entering their channels. It was a trade not without risks and one that led to the development of a keen rivalry between the various groups of pilots. Sleek schooners evolved, some which looked not unlike the famous cup yacht *America.* These fast sailing craft each carried a group of pilots, often a great many miles off shore in their search for vessels that were approaching the shipping channels. When such a vessel was located, a pilot then had to be placed on board. This was frequently a very dangerous transfer, especially in bad weather, from the small boat carried on the pilot schooner.

Foreign vessels were required to engage a pilot while American coasting vessels were not. All year long, throughout the worst of weather, the pilots had to be on station. Their vessels had to be constructed so they were as seaworthy and weatherly as possible. Never-the-less, through collision, stranding and simply being overcome in wild weather, schooners and pilots were lost. A pilot had to serve a long period of apprenticeship before he was finally licensed to carry out his profession. Once placed upon the deck of an arriving or departing vessel, he carried an enormous responsibility.

Near the turn of the century, New York and New Jersey combined their operations into one organization called the United New York and New Jersey Pilot's Association. Also close to that time, as had happened in so many places throughout the world, sail was giving way to steam and the beautiful pilot schooners gave way to power; first to steam and finally to diesel engines.

The seaward approaches to New York harbor were often fraught with many dangers to the mariner. Even Long Island Sound could deal a deadly blow upon occasion. Over many years it had earned the nickname "the Devil's belt" from sailors who had been caught in the sudden squalls or northeast gales that could turn the sound into a cauldron of rough, choppy seas. A vessel thrown against the northern shores of the sound generally found itself "on the rocks". The southern shore on the Long Island side was often sandier but both shores could be dangerous places for passing sailing craft.

Fog was another problem encountered in confined areas. In the "old days," navigational aids were not as sophisticated as they are today and skippers of sailing coastal vessels had to be well acquainted with the areas that they were navigating. Also, the closer one got to port, the more crowded became the places one had to sail through and collisions from one cause or another became common.

During the 1800's, the numbers of vessels being cast ashore on the approaches to New York continued to rise. The lives lost, the human suffering involved and the huge amount of money lost was soon being brought to the attention of the United States Congress.

Maritime losses were something in which almost everyone was interested. Many of the people who were living on or near the coast had come to accept these losses as a fact of life, but in few cases were they taken lightly. In December of 1836, the wrecks of the ships *Mexico* and *Brazil,* caused a great public outcry. Each vessel was carrying around 200 immigrants bound for the United States. One ship struck east of Rockaway and the other east of Jones Inlet, Long Island. Only a handful from each vessel survived. There were other such tragedies that imflamed the public but unfortunately, government action was slow.

In 1848, a life saving station was built at Sandy Hook. In 1849, some New York residents formed a state organization to build ten structures on or near Long Island to serve as relief houses for shipwrecked mariners but the locations were unmanned.

Finally in 1854, the United States Government authorized funds for paid keepers to man the stations and for the construction of six new buildings. Up until this time, the operation of each station had been entirely on a voluntary basis.

It wasn't until 1871 that the crews at the various stations were paid a salary and were kept on duty at a fixed level during the most dangerous months of the year. Mr. Sumner I. Kimball was appointed to be head of the Revenue Marine Bureau in 1871. This bureau had charge of the Life Saving Service. Mr. Kimball at once set about re-organizing the service. Each important station was equipped with a large surf boat capable of going out through very rough surf. In addition, each crew had at its disposal, the gear necessary to fire a line to a stranded vessel so a breeches buoy apparatus could be set up to rescue the passengers and crew, if the use of the surf boat was deemed impractical. Beach patrols were inaugurated during the bad months to look for stranded ships and to warn off with Coston flares any who ventured to close to the beach for their safety.

Above: The schooner barge *Imperial* stranded at Cedar Creek, New Jersey together with the steamer *Santuit* which was towing her in dense fog on April 1, 1896. The steamer worked off the beach but the barge was stuck fast. Life Savers landed the crew of five using the breeches buoy. The wreck was turned over to the Chapman Wrecking Company but was a total loss. **Below:** On July 4, 1896, a tow consisting of the steamer *Nottingham* and three coal laden barges stranded late in the evening off Southhampton Beach near Shinnecock Inlet, Long Island in dense fog. The tug managed to free herself and another barge but the *Central Railroad of New Jersey No. 6,* was hard aground. The third barge broke in half and was abandoned. Wreckers from the Chapman Wrecking Company managed to free the No. 6 about a week later and she was towed to Providence, Rhode Island.

In 1878, Mr. Kimball encouraged Congress to establish the United States Life Saving Service as a separate entity with himself as its one and only general superintendent. By that year, each station was manned by a crew of well trained men who had become experts in dealing with the surf and the shallow shore areas near their stations. Over the years the service was extended, in numbered districts, to cover almost the entire shoreline of the United States.

By the year 1900, the third district of the Life Saving Service contained 41 stations which were located along its shores. Eight of these were located in the state of Rhode Island; three being on Block Island, and the other 33 were placed along the shores of Long Island, New York.

The fourth district, which was located along the shores of New Jersey had 42 stations. Together, these two districts during the fiscal year 1899- 1900 played a role in going to 97 marine disasters in which ten vessels were total wrecks but in which only four lives were lost. This was indeed a tremendous difference from the preceding decades. The U.S. Life Saving Service continued to be active until 1915 when it and the U.S. Revenue Cutter Service were incorporated into the newly formed United States Coast Guard.

However, in spite of the pilots, the Life Saving Service, all the light houses, charts and buoys, the violent storms of winter cast many laboring vessels onto surf covered beaches where they were pounded to pieces; often in a very short period of time. Fog and tricky eddies added to the toll of losses, and collisions frequently occurred in crowded harbor areas. They still account for some disasters. Fire too, occasionally added to the lists of lost ships. In spite of all of man's best efforts, the water routes that made up the approaches to New York were able to exact over the years a heavy toll of ships and men's lives. Even the calmer waters within the harbor itself often reflected the ugly reality of shipwreck.

The United States Life Saving Service performed their duties with exemplary heroism along the shorelines of the country. In the photograph above the life-savers are landing their boat in the surf with a group on shore assisting. The man on the stern handles the steering oar. This was usually the keeper or number one surfman at the station.

Above: On July 30, 1896, about one year after the *Olinda* (page 18) was wrecked, the steamer *Tillie* ran aground at the same place - the rocks off Goose Hummock on the south side of Fisher's Island. The ship was under charter and was loaded with sardines. Tugs pulled her off two days later. The *Tillie* was later sunk while carrying munitions to the army at Cuba. **Below:** The steamer *Rosedale* was in a collision with a New York ferryboat on September 3, 1896 in the East River. She had 150 passengers who were all rescued. The accident occurred at noon. The Chapman Wrecking Company raised the vessel the next day and beached her at Astoria, Long Island.

Steamboat "Rosedale"
Sunk on Reef foot Broome St. E.R. Sept. 3D 1896.
Raised by Chapman Derrick & Wrecking Co.

Above: The ferryboat *Hackensack* hit the Middle Ground reef, one mile east of Hell Gate on February 12, 1897 during a thick snow storm and stove a large hole in her bottom. The vessel was refloated on the 15th by the Merritt & Chapman Wrecking company and towed to the 7th Street, East River dry-dock for repairs. **Below:** The steamer *Ulster* of the Saugerties Evening Line ran hard on the bank of the Hudson River on November 12, 1897. This was a strange accident where the pilot had stomach seizures and let go of the wheel. The vessel yawed around and ran on the bank at full speed.. She later sank by the stern. The *Ulster* was ultimately raised and repaired. She later returned to service on the river. Going by in the background is the steamer *Emeline* which appears later on in another accident on the Hudson River.

Above: Three people were drowned after a collision between the steamers *Catskill* and *St. John* in the North River on September 15, 1897. The *St. John* was coming down the river at about 7 p.m. when the accident occurred. After the collision, several craft gathered around the vessels to help save the passengers. The *Catskill* sank in about five minutes near the Jersey Shore. **Below:** The Merritt & Chapman Derrick and Wrecking Company raised the steamer and placed her on the flats at Weehawken on Sept. 18th.

STEEL SHIP "TROOP"
STRANDED ON LONG ISLAND COAST
NEAR FORGE RIVER LIFE S.S. STATION

MAY 24TH 1898

The British ship *Troop* came ashore in fog on the Great South Beach of Long Island near Moriches Inlet on May 24, 1898. The Life Savers from the Forge River station rigged the breeches buoy but the crew would not come ashore because sea conditions were calm. Wreckers refloated the vessel eleven days later and took her to New York City. *Photo from the collection of Capt. W.J.L. Parker, U.S.C.G. [Ret.]*

S. B. "CITY OF WORCESTER"
SUNK IN NEW LONDON HARBOR MAY 29ᵗʰ 1898

Above: The *City of Worcester* of the Norwich Line hit Cormorant Reef off New London, Connecticut on May 28, 1898. The vessel came into the harbor where she sank. Her passengers were removed and the vessel was later pumped out and refloated six days later. **Below:** The wrecking cranes were called on to handle some bizarre accidents. The driver of the Mutual Milk and Cream Co. truck probably ran off the end of a dock or ferry boat when the brakes failed. The salvage of the vehicle was necessary to keep the water clear for ships to lay alongside the pier. The salvage required a diver to go down and rig the slings for the derrick to pick up the truck.

Above: The schooner barge *E. W. Stetson* was built in Maine in 1862. She stranded in the great gale of November 27, 1898 near Jamesport, Long Island. **Below:** The coal barge *Independent* came ashore at Riverhead, Long Island in the same storm as the *Stetson*. The vessel was not seriously damaged and was towed off later. She was lost with all hands on Nov. 14, 1908, off Hog Island, Virginia.

Above: On February 11, 1899, during coaling operations at the White Star Line Pier, the British Steamer *Germanic* took a heavy starboard list because of the tons of ice on the decks and rigging. This allowed water to enter through the coal ports and she sank beside the dock. **Below:** She lay on the bottom for ten days before being refloated by the Merritt & Chapman Derrick & Wrecking Company. The main deck from the engine room aft was under water. This damaged the furniture and fittings as well as the cargo.

Above: The schooner barge *David Crockett* was forced by heavy ice on to Flynn's Knoll at the entrance to New York harbor on February 14, 1899. Wreckers worked on the hull for two weeks but they could not save it. The vessel was a total loss. **Below:** On March 23, 1899, the British bark *La Escocesa* alongside the tug *McCaldin Bros.* was flipped over by a strong gust of wind in upper New York bay. Both the bark and the tug sank. A week later, salvage crews raised the two vessels.

Above: On June 8, 1899, two New Haven Line steamers collided in the fog. The *Richard Peck* rammed the *C.H. Northam* in Long Island Sound and the *Northam* was beached to prevent her from sinking. Later refloated and repaired, the vessel was back on her run in three weeks. Below: The steamship *Leona* arrived in New York City on October 5, 1899. The vessel had sailed from Galveston with a cargo of 8,000 bales of cotton, rags and jute. When she arrived at the pier, the New York fire engines were called to help put out a fire in her holds. Harbor fire boats and land engines could not extinguish the flames and the vessel sank beside the dock. Divers and wreckers were at work for the next few weeks but the cargo, valued at $206,000 was a total loss.

Above: The steamer *Gate City* of the Savanah Line was bound for Boston on February 8, 1900, when she ran ashore at Moriches, Long Island, in dense fog. Life Savers removed 48 persons from the grounded vessel. Salvors saved part of her cargo but the ship had split in half and was a total loss. **Below:** The four masted British ship *County of Edinburgh* lost her way and ran aground near Squan Beach, New Jersey on February 12, 1900. Life Savers from the Squan Beach Life Saving Station assisted the crew and delivered messages to the wrecking company. The ship lay easy in the surf and no storms occurred. She was refloated on the 25th and towed to New York.

Above: A fire on the dock at Constable Hook, New Jersey spread to the full rigged ship *Josephus* during the night of May 7, 1900. The vessel was extensively damaged before fire fighters could bring the flames under control. **Below:** Two of the three masts were destroyed in the fire as well as all of the rigging. The cabin was gutted and the hold filled with water. The hull was sold on June 20th for $6,000 to Michael O'Donnell of Brooklyn. The vessel was converted to a three masted schooner barge. This view on deck shows salvage men at work cleaning up the mess after the ship had cooled down.

Above: A view looking aft on the burned out ship *Josephus* showing the charred rigging laying on deck. The fire gutted the entire ship fore and aft and left only the mizzen mast standing. **Below:** Another accident occurred later, after the ship was converted to a barge. She sank in the Lower Bay but was raised and repaired. The *Josephus* was finally lost to fire when she burned at Scotland, Virginia on April 4, 1924, along with the barge *Sea King*.

Above: Three liners of the North German Lloyd lines were lost to fire at their docks at Hoboken, New Jersey on June 30, 1900. The *SS Bremen, SS Saale,* and the *SS Main* were lost in the conflagration. The blaze started on the piers and spread rapidly engulfing the three ships. **Below:** The *Main* and the *Bremen* were beached at Hoboken after the fires were put out. It was estimated that nearly 200 persons died in the flames.

On July 11, 1900, the steamer *Emeline* accidentally hit the dock at Newburgh on the Hudson River, 15 miles below Poughkeepsie. The vertical beam engine was caught on dead center and could not be reversed in time to avoid the ship ramming into the dock. This type of slip, while uncommon, was embarrassing to the engineer. The *Emeline* was later raised and repaired. *Photo courtesy of the Steamship Historical Society of America.*

Above: Whenever celebrations occur in the harbor, almost every steamer available is loaded to the gunnels with people and its full speed to the scene for the best view. This type of action creates shipwrecks. The steamers going at full speed are in danger of collisions, given the close proximity to each other. **Below:** The overloading of steamers was another danger often overlooked by steamboat inspectors. The steamer *Havana* was photographed on October 12, 1892 during a Columbus Day Marine Parade in New York harbor. The *Havana* was formerly the U.S. Stmr. *Cosmopolitan* which was built in 1860 at Green Point, New York. The dangers of overloading are obvious.

Two photographs, which were taken about 85 years apart, of the South Street area in New York. The top photo was taken about 1900. The forest of masts and rigging covers the buildings on the opposite shore. The bottom photo was taken about 1985 in approximately the same location. The Brooklyn Bridge is in the background but there are no masts to be seen except for the crane on the left and the small mast on the tugboat at the right.

The Fire Island lighthouse was built in 1858 to replace a smaller less powerful light. This light was considered important for vessels arriving from Europe and was the first land light seen by lookouts on ships. The light marks an approach to New York Bay.

Chapter Three

With the passage of the years following the War of 1812, the number of vessels arriving and departing from the port of New York increased. In those early days most inbound ship captains tried their best to assure a landfall during the hours of daylight. Frequently, due to poor navigational aids and equipment, many vessels that made arrivals at night ended their voyage most unhappily.

From the tip of Montauk Point, at the eastern end of Long Island, all the way along the southern shore to its western end, there was not a decent harbor of refuge to be found for a large vessel. There was really no safe place to run into until the entrance appeared for the port of New York.

Sandy Hook was a notorious and dangerous spit of land that ran several miles, as a finger pointing north, from the coast of New Jersey. It extended very close to the path of traffic trying to use the shipping channels just off of its northern tip. From very early colonial days, an approach to New York harbor had to be made with care and caution.

One of the original and longest lasting of the lighthouses constructed on the east coast of the United States, was built at Sandy Hook in 1764. Another famous light marked the eastern end of Long Island. This was Montauk Point light, which was erected in 1797. A lighthouse on Fire Island, along the south shore of Long Island, came into use in 1826.

At Cape May, the southern most part of New Jersey, a lighthouse was built in 1823. Twelve years later, in 1835, another light was constructed at Barnegat Inlet, 45 miles south of Sandy Hook Light. This Barnegat lighthouse was replaced by a much taller structure in 1859. The new light stood 175 feet above sea level and was the first land based light usually seen by inbound vessels that were approaching from the south.

As time went on, many lighthouses were constructed in and around the confines of Long Island Sound. Execution Lighthouse was built on Execution Rocks, off New Rochelle in 1867. This area derived its name from the fact that it was used as a site where colonial prisoners were chained to low lying rocks and left to drown on the incoming tide. These dastardly deeds being performed by the King's officials were, of course, stopped after our winning the Revolutionary War; however, the name for the rocky reef held fast, as did the bones of some of its victims, both ships and men.

Before 1789, individual coastal states maintained the navigational aids and there were no criteria in force. Consequently the maintenance and operations were inadequate for safety. The laws enacted by congress in 1789 created the U.S. Lighthouse Service to "support, maintain and repair the lighthouses, fog signals, beacons and buoys on the bays, inlets and harbors of the United States for the purpose of assisting the navigation and safety of marine traffic." Following the creation of the Lighthouse Service there was progress and rapid growth in navigational aids along the coast. This was carried out under the direction of an Undersecretary of the Treasury. There were many deficiencies, waste and political shortcomings that lasted into the middle of the 19th century. A change was demanded by shipping interests which led to a marked improvement. In 1852, a Lighthouse Board was created by Congress. The act stated:

"An act making appropriations for light-houses, light-boats, buoys, &c., the Secretary of the Treasury is authorized and required to cause a board to be convened at as early a day as may be practicable after the passage of that act, to be composed of two officers of the navy of high rank, two officers of engineers of the army, and such civil officer of high scientific attainments as may be under the orders or at the disposition of the Treasury Department, to inquire into the condition of the light-house establishment of the United States, and make a general detailed report and programme to guide legislation in extending and improving our present system of construction, illumination, inspection and superintendence."

Above: The five masted schooner *Nathaniel T. Palmer* stranded at Long Beach, New Jersey at 3 a.m. on March 11, 1901 in thick weather and rough seas. **Below:** Her crew of 12 men were landed by the Life Savers using the breeches buoy. The vessel lay on the beach for a little over a week before it was refloated. The *Nathaniel T. Palmer* was built in 1898 in Bath, Maine and her gross tonnage was 2,440.

With the enactment of this legislation a renaissance occurred along the coast and the worst lighthouse service in the world became the finest and continues to be so today. The new lighthouses that were erected were built with various designs to blend with the local landscape. They were built with stones, cast iron and bricks. Most of the structures built in the 19th century are historic landmarks today. The Lighthouse Board continued in control of all the U.S. lighthouses until 1910. By that time the lighthouses had been divided up into districts according to their location. In 1910, the board was changed to the Bureau of Lighthouses, under the Department of Commerce, to which lighthouses had been transferred in 1903. In 1939, by order of President Franklin D. Roosevelt, the operation of all United States lighthouses and aids to navigation were taken over by the United States Coast Guard.

Prior to the Coast Guard takeover, each lighthouse had been manned by an attendant who usually lived at the light with his family. It was the attendant, or "keeper", so called, who was responsible for keeping the light in proper repair and in continuous operation during the hours between sunset and daylight. The keepers were occasionally called "wickies" because some of their daytime hours were spent cleaning the wicks in the light towers. A clean wick always burned bright. Coast Guard crews replaced the "keepers" after 1939. Eventually many of the lighthouses were either abandoned or became automated with no personnel at the station. Many of today's lights are run by solar power and require only periodic maintenance.

While lighthouses did indeed give aid to the mariners who were navigating near our coastline, it was becoming evident by the 1820's that additional help was needed in special places. Stationing lights off shore in dangerous areas, both as a guide and a warning, was thought to be an improvement over shore lights and as a result, lightships began to appear permanently at certain locations.

An early lightship was anchored near Sandy Hook in 1823. Although its location was moved about somewhat, the name of the station remained the same until the Sandy Hook lightship was replaced by the Ambrose lightship in 1908. A lightship was established off Cape Hatteras at Diamond Shoals in 1824. In 1827, this lightship was driven ashore and wrecked. It wasn't replaced for seventy years. The government didn't want to spend money on such things at the time.

The Lighthouse Board took over control of the lightships after its formation in 1852. In 1867, they began numbering the lightships so as to make identification easier. The early lightships were wooden and had only their sails for use in moving about or, getting into a safe haven if they happened to be ripped free from their heavy anchors in a storm. The first lightships launched with engines were introduced in 1893. Unfortunately, the engines in the first three were so weak, they had to be towed by others to get to their stations. Later lightships had better engines installed that could move them along at about ten knots. Inevitably, with the march of progress, the equipment used on lightships was gradually upgraded with better lenses being used in the lamps. Fog horns were added in the 1890's and eventually wireless and radio beacons.

The radio beacons were found, in time, to work well - too well in one particular case. On May 15, 1934, the giant liner *Olympic,* a sister ship to the *Titanic,* was rushing through a thick fog on the track of a radio beacon that was being sent out by the Nantucket Lightship, # 117. The liner was heading in from Europe to New York and followed the beacon right into the helpless lightship, cutting her in two, which sent her to the bottom. Four of her crew members were drowned.

Lightships had more than their share of accidents. Being located often in dangerous places where traffic was heavy, they were frequently rammed by passing tows or vessels trying to get by in a fog. They were occasionally pulled free from their great anchors during a spell of terrible weather and then driven at the mercy of the elements to some wave washed beach. There were other times when they were simply overwhelmed and lost with all hands. Life on board a lightship could go from one extreme to another, being boring one day and the next day both dangerous and frightening.

The crews on the lightships were all male and were changed every so often so that boredom didn't set in to the point of despair. The crews had regular duties to perform each and every day but these efforts seldom lasted the entire day. As a result many of the crews took up hobbies such as whittling or making rattan baskets to help pass away the time aboard ship. The early baskets made by lightship crews bring huge prices in maritime auctions that are held today.

Over the years, lightships have been phased out of the service. Frequently, large, automated light buoys have taken their place at important stations. The Ambrose Lightship was removed from duty in 1967 and a Texas Tower type structure took its place. Fortunately for posterity, the lightship was taken to the South Street Seaport Museum where it was made available to the public. People could board the lightship and get some idea as to what life might have been like while serving on what some of the old crew members might have described as "sitting on a floating target".

Today, in spite of all of man's best efforts, ships still came to grief from one cause or another. True, the numbers of wrecks diminished with the passage of time as we moved into the 1900's but they still happened. Even with all of our modern technological advances, shipwrecks and sinkings still occur and lives are lost.

The steamer *Poughkeepsie* ran up on some rocks at Stony Point in the Hudson River, a few miles south of Haverstraw early in the morning of March 21, 1901. The passengers were all taken ashore. The vessel was refloated by the Merritt & Chapman Company. The salvage vessel Raymond is shown alongside taking the cargo out of the steamer to lighten her for refloating. This vessel burned on June 26, 1910 at Highland, New York.

Above: On March 26, 1901, the Norwegian steamer *Gwent* washed ashore two miles east of the Long Beach Life Saving Station, Long Island, in thick stormy weather.**Below:** The life saving crew went to the vessel by surfboat and removed seven passengers. The crew stayed with their ship and a wrecking company floated her on March 31st.

Above: The *U.S.S. Rawlins* caught fire in her hold on August 10, 1901 alongside the pier at Pacific Street in Brooklyn. The ship was flooded and sunk to put out the fire. Most of the cargo of hay, straw, bran, and oats was lost. Damage was set at $70,000. The American Wrecking company refloated the ship on the 23rd and it was dry docked for repairs. Some of the grain was taken out and dried. **Below:** The American schooner *A. R. Keene* stranded near the Point Lookout Life Saving Station on May 10, 1901. The life savers laid a shot line across her on their first attempt but the crew left the vessel in the ship's yawl and proceeded to row off shore. The Life Savers launched their lifeboat and safely landed the crew of seven men. The Merritt & Chapman Wrecking Company worked on the hull but it was a total loss. Vessel and cargo was valued at $30,000. The schooner was on a voyage from Zaza, Cuba to New York City with a cargo of cedar.

Above: The schooner *Mola* came ashore near Chadwick, New Jersey in dense fog on April 20, 1901. Gale winds and high surf pushed the vessel over the outer bar and she moved closer to shore. Surfmen from the Chadwick station set up the breeches buoy and brought the crew of eight men safely ashore. The schooner was refloated on May 9th and towed to New York City for repairs. **Below:** The salvage steamer *Resolute* is shown towing the three masted schooner *Henry H. Grant* into port floating on her cargo. This type of operation was routine. Storms at sea caused many schooners to be abandoned. They had to be towed out of the shipping lanes for safety to other vessels.

Above: The ferry *Northfield* of the Staten Island Transit Company was in collision with the ferry *Mauch Chunk* of the Central Railroad of New Jersey at six in the evening of June 14, 1901. The collision occurred at the Battery near the southern tip of Manhattan Island while the *Mauch Chunk* was entering her slip and the *Northfield* was leaving hers. After the accident the *Northfield* drifted up the East River and sank a half mile away off Pier 10. **Below:** In the photograph a diver is shown going down the side of the sunken ferry *Northfield* in preparation for salvage. Five passengers and several horses lost their lives in the mishap.

Above: The United States transport vessel *Ingalls* tipped over in the balance dry-dock in the Erie Basin on June 14, 1901. The vessel had been placed in the dock for repairs when the weight of the ship turned the dock over and it sank in 50 feet of water.**Below:** The Merritt & Chapman wrecking company raised the vessel on June 22nd. There was little damage to the ship.

Above: The Joy Line steamer *Old Dominion* ran aground in Long Island Sound near Rye, N.Y., in dense fog on July 6, 1901. There were 165 passengers asleep at the time of the accident. **Below:** When the vessel ran onto a rocky bottom she punched holes in her hull and had to be repaired. The ship was refloated a month later.

Above: The ship *Commodore T.H. Allen* with 84,000 cases of kerosene and wax on board went aground off Sandy Hook, New Jersey. Just after going ashore, she caught fire outside New York harbor on July 18, 1901 and was very nearly consumed by the flames. the ship had just left New York and was bound for Yokohama. New York fireboats and tugs came to her assistance and filled her with water. Much of the upper hamper of the ship was destroyed by the fire. The hull was refloated and towed to New York. She was later converted to a coal barge by the Baker Transportation Company and renamed *Sterling*. On January 9, 1912, she sprung a leak and sank off Block Island, Rhode Island. **Below:** Most of the fires in and around New York harbor were fought by the city's fireboats. The one above was tied up at the Battery. Several of the city's tugboats were able to join the fireboats in battling flaming ships and docks when fires occurred.

The schooner *Joseph I. Thompson* lost her rudder on July 24, 1901 while on route from Greenwich, Connecticut for New York City with a cargo of stone. She ran on the rocks near New Rochelle where she sank. The Merritt & Chapman Wrecking Company refloated the vessel on the 28th and towed her to City Island where the leak was repaired. She was then towed to Greenwich for further repairs.

Above: The schooner *Lucy W. Snow* came ashore in stormy weather at Moriches, Long Island on September 11, 1901. Life Savers from the Moriches station went to the aid of the stranded vessel and the keeper telegraphed for a wrecking tug. Attempts were made to haul the schooner off the beach but she was a total loss. **Below:** The schooner *Hannah F. Carleton* was bound from New York City for Bangor, Maine with 300 tons of soft coal on Setember 30, 1901 when she went aground on Flynn's Knoll in the Lower Bay off Sandy Hook, New Jersey. The Captain and crew were taken off by the Life Savers from the Sandy Hook Station. The vessel was full of water when the Merritt & Chapman Wrecking company derrick barge MONARCH floated her and brought the hull to the Erie Basin in Brooklyn.

Above: The British bark *Criffel* was loading cargo at Pier 12, East River when fire broke out in the hold near the main hatch on October 8, 1901. The crew scuttled the ship beside the pier to extinguish the fire. The strange looking boom across the center of the photograph is from a wrecking barge alongside. The *Criffel* was pumped out and floated on October 12th. Damage to her cargo was listed as $150,000. **Below:** The Merritt & Chapman wrecking tug *Resolute*. The galloping black horse flag is prominently displayed on the stack. The vessel is under power with a tow line out which probably means that she is trying to tow a vessel off the beach.

On the morning of October 22, 1901, the Jersey Central Railroad ferry *Elizabeth* caught fire in mid stream while on her run from New York City to Communipaw. She was towed to the Communipaw Flats where the fire burned itself out. There were no lives lost but the vessel was a total loss.

The German ship *Flottbek* out of Plymouth, England for New York City with a cargo of china clay and arsenic stranded on a bar at Monmouth Beach, New Jersey on November 24, 1901 in a strong gale with heavy surf.

Above: The Life Savers from the Monmouth Station went to their aid and landed the crew of twenty-four men by the breeches buoy. The Merritt & Chapman Wrecking Company was called to salvage the vessel. The cargo was unloaded onto barges and sent to New York. The vessel lay on the beach until December 17th when it was pulled off and towed to New York. **Below:** a photograph made on deck aboard the *Flottbek* shows the catwalks above the main deck which are used by crewmen in high seas to prevent being swept overboard.

Above: In a dense fog, the ferry *College Point,* a side wheel steamer built in 1868, ran aground on a ledge near North Brother Island in the East River on December 13, 1901. Other vessels nearby rescued the people on board and landed them at College Point. The ferry subsequently slid off the ledge into deep water. She was later raised by the Merritt & Chapman Wrecking Company. **Below:** The four masted steel hulled bark *Sindia* was fighting heavy weather on the night of December 15, 1901 off the coast of New Jersey when she stranded on the beach at Ocean City. Life Savers removed her crew by surfboat. Two days later, she filled with water and was abandoned to wreckers. The *Sindia* was bound from Kobe, Japan to New York with a cargo of Japanese porcelain, silk, camphor and linseed oil. Wreckers succeeded in salvaging part of her cargo but much of it is still buried under the sands off Ocean City. The loss was valued at $249,000. Occasionally there are plans set forth to salvage the rest of the cargo of Japanese porcelain aboard the hull of the ship which is now buried under a few feet of sand. The modern day value of the porcelain is in the millions of dollars.

One of the hobbies for tourists is post cards. Thousands of cards were made of various subjects in resort areas. The first cards were made through the photographic process and were sharp and clear reproductions. The later ones were screened half tones and were not as clear. Several of the early post cards were made from photographs of Life Saving Stations. The principal subject matter along the coastline was shipwrecks. The *Sindia* was an excellent motif for the postcard albums. The two post cards above are collectors items and can sometimes be bought in flea markets, but they are expensive.

On February 2, 1902, the full rigged ship *L. Shepp* of 1,850 tons, bound from Hong Kong to New York with a general cargo ran ashore at Point Lookout at Long Beach on Long Island. The accident report stated: "Ship became unmanageable during a strong westerly gale with a heavy sea and stranded 1,000 yards offshore, one mile southwest of Long Beach Life Saving Station." Four days later, wrecking crews managed to float the ship. She was towed, half full of water, to New York. Her cargo was badly damaged.

This photograph was taken aboard the *L. Shepp* and shows the difficulties crewmen had in handling a large sailing ship in the winter. The control lines for the sails are covered with snow and ice. Running a line through a pulley while it is iced up is practically impossible. The cold weather certainly did create problems for the deep water sailors.

Above: The schooner barge *Lichtenfels Bros.* sunk on Flynn's Knoll, Sandy Hook, New Jersey on the night of February 21, 1902, with the loss of four men. The barge left Norfolk two days earlier with a load of coal for Providence, Rhode Island. The vessel was a total loss. **Below:** On March 1, 1902, the British steamer *Acara* went ashore on Jones Inlet Bars off Jones Beach, New York. The stranding occurred at 2 a.m. during strong southwest winds with seas running high. Life Savers launched surfboats to go to the aid of the crew but two boats were launched from the wreck with 61 people aboard. One of these boats was a large lifeboat. This boat weathered the seas and landed in safety. The other, a smaller boat, capsized in the breakers spilling seventeen men into the water. Life Savers rescued these men and brought all hands to the station and cared for them. Part of the cargo of tea was saved but the hull was a total loss.

Chapter Four

Nearly two hundred years ago, with numerous maritime losses being reported, sometimes many on a weekly basis, there were those who managed to profit from the misfortunes of others. The rising tide of shipwrecks gave birth to a new profession along our coastline. The "wrecker" was found close to shore and ever on the watch for signs of a vessel cast up on the beach. If some unfortunate craft was sunk a little distance off shore, the wrecker didn't mind taking a bit of a risk to see what he could salvage for himself. Salvage without getting into trouble with the authorities was his aim. A wrecker wasn't as much interested in saving lives as he was in personal enrichment; at least not in the early days.

Back in the early half of the nineteenth century, shipwrecks along our Atlantic coastline were often considered a boon to the community. A stranded vessel that was breaking up in the surf, or would do so in the minds of many, was often viewed as "fair game". Its cargo and fittings were generally considered by some of the locals to be the property of the first to find and "latch on to it".

The coasts of Long Island and New Jersey certainly had their share of eager wreckers who were quick to grab up any material thrown up on the beach. Cargo and other materials from stranded ships quickly went into waiting horse drawn beach carts and hauled away to cellars, sheds or barns before wreck masters or insurance agents were able to arrive upon the scene.

Although this was regarded as blatant theft by some, the wreckers didn't think along those lines. It was looked upon by many of the latter as a God given bounty and the old saw of "finders keepers", was the motto that many lived by. Unfortunately, this attitude still held sway in some areas until well into the 1900's.

"Free" timber from a disintegrating ship was often used to add another room on the house or in building a new shed and if nothing else, it could be used for firewood during the winter. Paint from a stranded ship's paint locker was always welcome and rope from the running rigging could be used in many ways around the home or farm. If not useful at home, much of the salvaged material could always be turned into cash or traded for something that was useful.

From solitary individuals to groups who cooperated and worked together, the business of wrecking grew and finally led to the formation of some very large companies whose sole aim or major interest was the salvaging of ships and cargoes that had suffered mishap from the sea. One of the most famous and outstanding of these larger companies was the firm of Merritt, Chapman & Scott, whose offices were located for a long time at 17 Battery Place, in New York City.

All of the three partners in the firm of Merritt, Chapman & Scott, began their careers separately and independently. Captain Isreal J. Merritt was a man who had been much involved with salvage and shipwrecks for many years prior to the Civil War. In 1860, the Board of Marine Underwriters in New York, were very much concerned with the increasing number of shipwrecks and losses occurring along the nearby Atlantic coast. They also disliked the very poor way in which salvage work was being handled, so they formed the Coast Wrecking Company. They placed Captain Merritt in charge.

With a flag portraying a galloping black horse flying at their mastheads, the vessels of the Coast Wrecking Company became the salvors of a large number of vessels. They soon became widely known for their excellent work not only locally but in areas that were a considerable distance from New York.

It was Captain Merritt himself who established the galloping Black Horse as a house flag for the company. He chose this flag because he felt that it symbolized the agents who worked in the field for the company and who raced on horseback to get to the nearest telegraph station and inform the company as to the location of the latest wreck. The competition among wreckers was keen in years gone by and frequently, the first salvage outfit appearing upon the scene was the one hired to do the job.

Above: A view of the harbor taken around the turn of the century. The traffic consists of a couple of ferry boats, some small craft, a tug towing a three masted schooner and various other harbor craft plying their trades. There are several people lining the pier looking out at the traffic. **Below:** The wrecking steamer *Tasco* tied up at Cranes dry-dock at the Erie Basin in Brooklyn. The *Tasco* was built in 1907 for the T.A. Scott Company of New London. She was 109 feet long and measured 319 gross tons.

Within twenty years after the formation of the Coast Wrecking Company, Captain Merritt was able to buy out the ownership and he then changed the name to the Merritt Wrecking Company and went into partnership with his son Isreal, Jr.

In 1881, William E. Chapman, another New York operator, founded the Chapman Derrick and Wrecking Company of Brooklyn. By the 1890's, he was headquartered at 70 South Water Street in New York City. While harbor lighterage was an important part of his business, equally important was the salvage of wrecked vessels and cargoes. In addition to lighters, Chapman owned three huge derricks named "EDGAR", "RELIANCE" and "MONARCH". These goliaths could lift tremendously heavy objects off the bottom and soon became familiar to many coastal inhabitants who often watched as they pulled broken vessels up from the depths.

Often, both the Merritt and the Chapman firms would race each other to see who would be the first to get to a wreck. Hard feelings soon developed between the two companies. As luck would have it, both companies went to the aid of the eleven thousand ton American liner *St. Paul*, which stranded during a fog in January, 1896, off the coast of Long Branch, New Jersey. As a result of the altercation which followed, the two rivals wound up in court. It was finally decided by the insurance companies that both of the wrecking companies should work together to get the big liner refloated. This they were able to do. Putting their old differences behind them, the two organizations apparently saw the wisdom of a merger and in 1897, joined forces to become the Merritt & Chapman Derrick & Wrecking Company. The address for the new firm was located at 27 William Street in New York City.

In the fifteen or more years that followed the merger, Merritt & Chapman found itself involved with hundreds of marine wrecks and mishaps. It was constantly being called for its services. By 1915, the company had grown to the point where it owned seven wrecking steamers, five schooner rigged salvage barges plus a large fleet of derrick barges, pile drivers and an abundance of salvage and diving equipment. At that time, all of the divers were "hard hat" divers who depended for their air supply upon hand operated pumps that were worked from the surface. Also, by 1915, the headquarters for this company which still flew the Black Horse Flag, had been moved to 17 Battery Place. The warehouses and dock facilities had long before been located at Stapleton on Staten Island.

As Merritt & Chapman Derrick & Wrecking Company expanded its operations during and after World War One, it also began to work in close cooperation on many jobs with the T.A. Scott Company, a wrecking and salvage organization located at New London, Connecticut. It therefore did not come as a great surprise to many among the waterfront's best informed, when T.A. Scott merged with Merritt and Chapman in 1922. Captain T.A. Scott was elected to be the first president of the newly formed firm of Merritt, Chapman & Scott. Their business offices remained at the old address at 17 Battery Place.

Captain Thomas Albertson Scott was a man of undeniable courage and abilities. He was born in 1830, near Snow Hill, Maryland. In 1852, he signed on aboard the schooner *John Willetts* as an ordinary seaman. Within three years time he had advanced himself to the point where he was captain and part owner of his own schooner.

He eventually sold his interest in the schooner and he moved his family to Coytesville, New Jersey, where he tried his hand at running a general store. This apparently was something that did not appeal to the venturesome captain, for less than two years later he had accepted a contract to do salvage work on the cargo of a steamer that had recently sunk near Fort Lee, New Jersey. He was subsequently involved in several salvage efforts in and around the New York area while he was master of the tug *Reliance*, which belonged to the Off Shore Wrecking Company.

On January 30, 1879, he established his reputation for personal courage when he jammed his own body into a hole that had been cut in the side of the New York ferry boat *Union* by a passing tug. The *Union* was in the Hudson River at the time and the rapid inrush of icy water was threatening to sink both the ferry and its crowd of terrified passengers. His heroic efforts were successful but his actions cost the captain a badly lacerated right arm, much loss of blood, some broken ribs and a lengthy stay in the hospital.

Around 1871, Captain Scott was hired to build the Race Rock Lighthouse by a man named Francis Hopkinson Smith. The lighthouse was to be located on Fisher's Island off the shores of Connecticut. Captain Scott moved his family to New London so they could all be together while he was working on this most difficult job. The lighthouse was finally finished in 1878. No doubt, it was

Above: Two schooner barges were wrecked on Romer Shoals on March 5, 1902. Both barges were converted deep water sailing ships, the ex bark *P.J. Carleton* on the left and the ex ship *Ringleader* on the right. The barges were in the tow of the tug *Richmond*, bound from Newport News, Virginia, to Boston, Massachusetts with large cargoes of coal. They went aground a mile north of Flynn's Knoll off Sandy Hook, New Jersey. Both barges were a total loss. **Below:** The schooner barge *Narragansett* was built in 1866 as the side wheel steamer *Manatus*. Rebuilt as a barge in 1901, she was hit in the stern by an unknown vessel. The cut does not appear to go below the water line but extensive repairs had to be made to make her seaworthy again. The tug coming alongside is the *Guiding Star.*

while he was working on the lighthouse construction that Captain Scott envisioned the opportunities available to anyone opening a wrecking company at New London.

In 1903, his wrecking and salvage company was officially opened under the name T.A. Scott Company, Inc. It was located at 292 Pequot Avenue on the banks of the Thames River. It was close to the entrance of the river, which flowed past New London on its way into Long Island Sound. Captain Scott's home was located a very short distance from where his warehouse and dock facilities were built and over the years these waterfront sites became a source of much public interest.

In addition to his other skills, Captain Scott was an able "hard hat" diver and he personally conducted an underwater survey of the sunken hull of the steamer *City of Columbus,* under conditions that were then described as "terrible". The steamer had struck on Devil's Bridge off the coast of Martha's Vineyard during the month of January, 1884. There was much loss of life and the few who did survive suffered greatly while clinging to the steamer's icy rigging. Captain Scott did his survey in the rough, frigid waters very shortly after the wreck occurred.

Captain Scott lost his eldest son when during salvage operations on the sound steamer *Narragansett,* the young man was swept away from the jibboom of their salvage schooner during a wild, wave tossed night and his body was never recovered. The captain and his family lamented this grievous loss for a long period of time.

A newspaper article written about the captain in March, 1898, shed some interesting light on the history of the company. It stated that Captain Scott's record book, going back over four years, indicated that his company had been active in the salvage of 33 wrecks per year. His warehouse gradually became adorned with dozens of the quarterboards, or nameboards from many of the stricken vessels that he had worked on. Inside the warehouse and strewn about in the surrounding area were countless relics from many of these lost ships.

The T.A. Scott Company grew steadily as time went on and it became one of the largest salvage outfits located at the eastern end of Long Island Sound. Their large 109 foot steam powered lighter and salvage vessel *Tasco* was built for Captain Scott at New London in 1907. It became part of a growing fleet of tugs, pile drivers and barges that were in constant use by his company.

Unfortunately, Captain Scott died in 1907. His son, Captain Thomas Albertson Scott, Jr., born in 1877, while the family was living in Connecticut, took over control of the business following his father's death. Under the younger Scott's control, the company continued in salvage work but also expanded into more general construction activities. In 1911, the T.A. Scott Company took over control of the Boston Tow Boat Company and further enhanced their abilities.

During World War One, in 1917, Captain Scott joined the United States Navy. He was then put in charge of all government salvage work carried on in U.S. waters. From 1918 to 1920, Captain Scott served as a member of the United States Shipping Board.

After leaving the Shipping Board in 1920, he re-entered the T.A. Scott Company and was again elected as its president, a position which he had resigned in 1917. In 1922, the T.A. Scott Company merged with the Merritt & Chapman Company forming one of the biggest salvage and construction firms on the east coast.

The operations at the Scott yard at New London were greatly reduced after 1925. The huge, wooden, World War One built tug *Guardsman* caught fire and burned at the dock on New Year's Eve, 1924. The tug was scuttled to extinguish the fire but was eventually raised and sold out of the company. Interestingly, the property at 292 Pequot Avenue was still listed as belonging to Merritt, Chapman & Scott in the 1955 issue of Merchant Vessels of the United States.

Captain Scott continued in active service with the company until he was retired as honorary chairman in 1951. He died in 1961. Mr. Louis E. Wolfson, who had been elected to the board of Merritt, Chapman & Scott in 1949, followed Captain Scott as chairman in 1951. Mr. Wolfson was elected president of the company in 1953, a position he held until 1959.

During the later years of the company's operations it had expanded to the point where it possessed a very large fleet of vessels that could and did operate anywhere along our coast and in addition also operated a large branch on the Great Lakes. The company had, over the years, even conducted salvage operations as far afield as the Caribbean. Also, during the later years, the main offices had been moved "up town" and were located at 260 Madison Avenue near the middle of Manhattan Island.

Above: The Nova Scotia barkentine *Persia* stranded near Long Beach on March 16, 1902. The weather was thick with a strong southeast wind blowing. Life Savers landed the crew of ten with the breeches buoy. The vessel suffered damage to her rigging and the hull had a pronounced hog. Wreckers floated the *Persia* ten days later. The ship was of 598 tons, bound from Buenos Aires to New York with a cargo of hides. **Below:** The tug *John A. Hughes* and the schooner barge *Mabel L. Phillips* both went aground on Lloyd's Neck, Long Island in a storm on the morning of November 26, 1902. The falling tide left the tugboat high and dry. Both vessels were later successfully hauled off the beach by the Merritt & Chapman Wrecking Company and towed to New York.

Above: The French bark *Olivier de Clisson* grounded at Point Lookout on Long Island on February 8, 1903 in strong winds and high seas. A Life Saver walking his beach patrol signaled the vessel with Coston signals but the ship ignored the flares and went ashore on high water. The vessel was under the command of the first officer at the time, as the Captain had died at sea during the passage from Plymouth to New York. The Life Savers landed the crew. The Merritt & Chapman Wrecking Company began work and unloaded the cargo of china clay. The bark was pulled off the beach on February 12th and towed to Stapleton, Staten Island. **Below:** The American schooner *John F. Kranz* came ashore at Mantoloking, New Jersey on March 21, 1903 during high winds and rough surf. The crew of eight was saved by the Life Savers. The cargo of logwood was saved but the vessel was a total loss. The main mast broke in two half way up from the deck.

Above: The British steamer *Joseph Merryweather* was in a collision with the German steamship *Alleghany* during thick fog in New York Harbor on April 8, 1903. The collision tore a large hole in the starboard side of the German vessel. The watertight compartments kept her from sinking entirely and she was raised by the Merritt & Chapman Wrecking Company and taken to the Erie Basin. She sailed on April 28th for Port Limon. The *Joseph Merryweather* sailed on the 25th after repairs to her stem. **Below:** The Italian bark *Angela E. Maria* was destroyed by an explosion and fire on July 30, 1903. The ship was being loaded with petroleum and naptha when the accident occurred at the oil docks at Constable Hook at Bayonne, New Jersey. Several of the crew were injured in the fire. The heavily laden ship burned for hours and illuminated the upper bay area of New York. The burning hulk was towed away from the dock and moored in the middle of the bay. Cause of the explosion was reported in the paper as: "An overpowering desire for baked bologna sausage on the part of the crew, caused the cook to go below and start to bake with the galley stove." The explosion occurred when the flames from the stove ignited the naptha fumes. The hull was later converted to a barge.

Above: A continuing problem for salvagers was sunken schooners. Sometimes they could be saved and sometimes not. The three master *Nellie T. Morse,* 459 tons out of Rockland, Maine, sank in 1902. She was built in 1879 and was a total loss. These types of vessels usually lasted about 20 years. Several lasted much longer when they avoided being sunk or run aground. **Below:** The *Annie E. Webb,* 101 tons and registered in New York sank in 1904. She was built in 1876 and was raised to sail again from this mishap.

Above: On August 29, 1903, the British ship *Charles S. Whitney* grounded at the Execution Rocks Lighthouse in Long Island Sound. The Merritt & Chapman Wrecking Company worked to refloat the ship but she developed leaks and could not be moved with five feet of water in her hold. **Below:** The salvagers removed her cargo and pulled her free. The vessel was towed to New York and hauled out on dry-dock for conversion to a schooner barge.

Above: There were some anxious moments following the wreck of the *Erastus Corning* on Copp's Rocks outside Norwalk Harbor on December 24, 1903. The vessel was off her course by two or three miles when the accident occurred. Passengers were ordered into life boats, some with only flimsy night clothes, and then ordered back aboard when it was determined that the vessel would not sink. One lifeboat however broke away and drifted ashore. The occupants were assisted by shoreside parties and no one was lost. Other passengers aboard the wreck were taken off by small boats. The steamer was refloated by the Merritt & Chapman Wrecking Company on December 29th and towed to New York by the steamer *Hustler*. **Below:** Another unexplained collision in the Lower Bay occurred on February 1, 1904. The British steamer *Boston City* while proceeding up the Lower Bay was run into by the Wilson Line steamer *Colorado*. The British vessel was piloted into shallow water to prevent her from sinking. The *Colorado* rescued some of the crew of the *Boston City* and then proceeded to her dock. After her cargo was taken out, the steamer, sunk to her decks, was later refloated by the Merritt & Chapman Wrecking Company.

Above: The Joy Line steamship *Tremont* was destroyed by fire on February 8, 1904, while tied to the pier in New York City. The fire broke out early in the morning and one man was lost in the flames. Two trained lions and a dog which were aboard as cargo were also lost. **Below:** This type of fire attracted both land and sea firefighters who have an unlimited supply of water. The result was a sunken hull with a heavily damaged superstructure. The hull was later raised by the Merritt & Chapman Wrecking Company but was a total loss.

The General Slocum

Above: On June 15, 1904, the steamer *General Slocum* left the 3rd street dock and headed up the East River for a Sunday school outing with 1,358 passengers, most of whom were children. Fire broke out on board the vessel and could not be controlled. *Drawing by Paul C. Morris* **Below:** In one of history's worst marine disasters, 1,031 lives were lost that day. The hull sank off Hunt's Point in the East River. Subsequent investigations turned up gross violations of all safety rules and substandard fire fighting equipment on board the excursion vessel of the day.

Above: The Merritt & Chapman Wrecking Company, using four derricks, raised the burned out hull of the *General Slocum*. **Below:** She was towed to a shipyard and converted to a coal barge. The barge named *Maryland* was lost in 1912 off New Jersey.

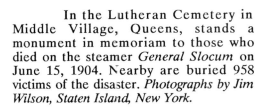

In the Lutheran Cemetery in Middle Village, Queens, stands a monument in memoriam to those who died on the steamer *General Slocum* on June 15, 1904. Nearby are buried 958 victims of the disaster. *Photographs by Jim Wilson, Staten Island, New York.*

The worst marine disaster in New York occurred on June 15, 1904, when the steamer *General Slocum* burned with the loss of 1031 persons near Hell Gate. Most of those that died were women and children. The ship was on an annual excursion cruise for the Sunday school classes of St. Marks German Lutheran Church. The disaster was caused by an explosion in the cookstove. The flames spread among the dry wooden beams of the ship covered with many coats of old paint, fanned by a brisk head-on breeze. Soon the entire ship was an inferno and hysteria spread among the passengers. The panic drove people over the side to escape the flames. Most of these drowned or were crushed under the churning paddle wheels. The captain became alarmed and conned his ship full speed up the river to a remote area off North Brother Island, killing scores in his flight.

The aftermath of the tragedy was shocking. The captain was arrested as were many others, including crewmen, safety inspectors and company officials. Charges were brought on and leveled at all hands. The only man convicted, however, was Captain William Van Schaick. He received a ten-year sentence for manslaughter but was pardoned after serving only two years. The claims against the owners of the *General Slocum* arising from the deaths amounted to $1,475,673. This also included $950 for the city of New York for the draping of City Hall. President Theodore Roosevelt personally participated in the firing of many marine inspectors after the *Slocum* disaster. The standards for steamboats were upgraded and improved each year afterward and then enforced diligently. Not only by inspectors but by passengers too. Periodically, masters and owners were in court and were fined for laxity in safety rules. Legal compliance became more complex as years passed causing the expense of running vessels to grow with each new rule but boat travel became safer. In later years, older steamboats were retired to the shipbreakers and were not replaced. The burned out hull of the *Slocum* was raised by wreckers and converted to a coal barge. The vessel was finally lost on December 14, 1912 when it foundered in a storm off Atlantic City, New Jersey.

Above: Winter ice was the cause of numerous accidents and sinkings in and around New York harbor. On January 5, 1904, the three masted schooner *Charles K. Buckley* was crushed by ice and sank on her cargo of lumber. She was raised and repaired. **Below:** The Pilot Boat *Ambrose Snow #2* on station off Sandy Hook during a heavy blow and moderate seas. The life of a New York pilot was difficult when the wind picked up the waves. Pilots had to transfer to larger vessels using small boats and Jacob's ladders. It was not an easy profession.

Above: The Parrsboro, Nova Scotia, schooner *Nellie I. White* went ashore at Lloyds Neck on Long Island on June 8, 1904, loaded with lumber. Grounding like this were rather common in winter but the Captain lost his way in an early summer fog. **Below:** The Merritt & Chapman Wrecking company brought a lighter alongside and unloaded the schooner in preparation for refloating.

Schr. "NELLIE I. WHITE"
Ashore at Llyods' Neck L.I. Sound, - June 9-1904.

Ferry Boat "COLUMBIA"

Above: The ferry *Columbia* of the Wall Street line was in collision with the sound steamer *City of Lowell* in dense fog on the morning of November 4, 1904. All of the passengers aboard the vessel were rescued but ten horses were drowned. The *Columbia* was refloated by the Merritt & Chapman Wrecking Company on November 8th and repaired. **Below:** On November 13, 1904, the ferry *Port Morris* was blown ashore in gale winds a half mile west of Berrians Island in the East River. The vessel was high and dry on the rocks and suffered some damage. She was later refloated by the Merritt & Chapman Wrecking Company and continued in service.

Above: On December 26, 1904, the British steamer *Drumelzier* stranded on Fire Island bar off Long Island at 3 a.m., during a blinding snow storm. Gusty northeast winds and heavy surf hampered life saving efforts. The ship lay on the bar for four days and was finally abandoned when high seas endangered the crew. Life Savers rescued the men with lifeboats and the ship was a total loss. **Below:** The British steamer *Indus* came ashore at Fire Island, abreast of the lighthouse in dense fog on January 12, 1905. She had sailed from Havana Cuba for New York with a cargo of sugar. Life Saving crews from the Fire Island and Point of Woods stations made repeated trips through heavy surf to assist the vessel. After much of her cargo was jettisoned, she was refloated on the 15th and steamed to New York. The *Indus* was engaged in the coolie trade and carried more lifeboats than a conventional freighter. *Photos by Anderson, courtesy of the Suffolk Marine Museum, West Sayville, New York.*

Above: On December 17, 1905, the schooner *Belle O'Neill* was flying a flag of distress while 300 miles southeast of Sandy Hook, New Jersey. The schooner was on a voyage from Georgetown, South Carolina for New York with a load of lumber. Shortly afterward, the yacht *Niagara* from New York went alongside and towed the schooner into Hampton Roads. **Below:** The schooner *Bessie Whiting* with a load of lumber from Port Royal, South Carolina for New York, was in collision on the morning of December 27, 1906 with two mud scows off the Sandy Hook lightship. The two scows were overturned while the schooner suffered a large hole in the starboard side of the bow. The schooner sunk on her cargo and was later towed into New York by the tug McCaldin Bros.

Above: The British steamer *Cearense,* while battling a snowstorm, came ashore near Toms River, New Jersey on March 16, 1906 at 4:20 a.m. It was soon discovered by the men from the Life Saving Station. The Life Savers fired a shot line out to the vessel but later it was decided to bring the 21 passengers ashore with life boats. Everyone was landed safely. The vessel was towed off after the cargo was lightered. **Below:** The Norwegian steamer *Bodo* went ashore on March 20, 1906 at Jones Inlet on Long Island, ten miles from Sandy Hook during thick weather. The Captain and crew were rescued by the Life Savers. The Merritt & Chapman Wrecking Company went to work on the vessel. Her cargo of bananas had to be thrown overboard to lighten the ship which was refloated on March 27th.

One of the grand Cunard Liners admired by New Yorkers was the four stacker *Mauretania*. She was built in 1907 at Newcastle, England and was a sister ship to the ill fated Lusitania, torpedoed by a German Submarine. The *Mauretania* was 762 feet long and was registered as 30,704 gross tons. She could do 27 knots by using her 68,000 h.p. steam engines. She held the transAtlantic record for twenty years, crossing in four and one half days at 27 knots. She was used as a troopship in the first World War. The liner was scrapped at Rosyth, Scotland in 1935. She is shown leaving New York Harbor with the aid of Moran Tugs. *Photo by Edward Viez, courtesy of the Steamship Historical Society of America.*

Chapter Five

If one had to enumerate the various sizes and types of the many vessels that were leaving, entering and operating in and around New York harbor, the list would be a surprisingly long one. Basically we can divide those vessels into about four main groups.

In the first group would be the large deep sea travelers from all over the world. The vessels comprising the second category would be those involved in the coasting trade, both large and small, that were entering or leaving from east coast ports of the United States or from the Maritime Provinces of Canada. The third group on our list would be made up of those medium sized and smaller vessels that largely accounted for much of the hustle and bustle that constantly went on in and around New York harbor. These can simply be categorized as harbor craft of many diverse types. The fourth class of vessels and distinct unto themselves were the many fishing boats that came and went from places like the Fulton Fish Market on South Street where fresh fish were brought in daily.

Up until the 1800's, sail was the motivating power for all of the vessels navigating our eastern waters. The earliest visitors to our shores sailed in small galleons whose size was not much different than some of the fishing vessels that arrived at Fulton Fish Market. Many of the mariners of the early 1600's made some marvelously long voyages in vessels barely 60 or 70 feet in length. During the 1700's, ships visiting New York gradually increased in size but the vast majority of the vessels arriving in America were foreign built. The colonists were, by English law, not encouraged to build large ships. Cargoes headed for overseas shipment were required to be carried in hulls that had been constructed in the mother country; namely England. The colonists did build small coasting vessels enabling them to get produce and goods to and from large ports but it wasn't until after the Revolutionary War that shipbuilding in the United States got going on a large scale.

By the time fleet clipper ships were being launched in the U.S. in the late 1840's and early 1850's, New York had become famous as a producer of fast sailing vessels. Even Donald McKay, the celebrated Boston builder of clippers got his training at a yard in New York. Yards owned by people such as William H. Webb, Jacob A. Westervelt and others were located on the East River in New York. Many of these clipper ship builders got their start constructing deep water sailing vessels by building the earlier packets that ran to Europe and back on fixed schedules.

Following the clippers, many of the famous "down easters" were to be seen loading and unloading at wharves along the Hudson and East Rivers. These lofty windjammers were built in New England and were the last of the American square rigged, deep water, sailing ships to battle the gales off Cape Horn.

The mid 1800's also saw steam vessels cutting into trades previously controlled by sailing vessels. Steamboat transportation of coastal passengers was one particularly important change in traveling habits that was manifested on the New York waterfront. Many of the early coastal steamers were wooden side wheelers burning wood for fuel and carrying both freight and passengers on some of the more protected routes to and from New York. Many of these vessels were built in New York, Brooklyn and Greenpoint.

It wasn't long after the coastal steamers had proven themselves that they began to extend their trips. Soon longer deep water voyages were being made by steam propelled vessels that sailed from foreign ports. By the turn of the century, giant liners had control of the passenger trade and sailing vessels were gradually fading from the waterfront scene.

Schooner operation in our coastal trade went on for a long time, outlasting the use of deep water square rig for twenty or more years. Schooners, both large and small could be seen at New York wharves right up until World War Two. Many smaller schooners were built in and around the New York area. There were builders such as J.M. Bayles & Son, who operated from 1863 until 1891, and John R. Mather who built vessels from 1838 to 1884. Both had yards in Port Jefferson, Long Island and added a large number of small two and three masted schooners to fleets hailing from New York and areas nearby. Literally hundreds of small sloops and schooners were set afloat from yards in New York, Long Island, Connecticut and New Jersey. Most were built for a particular trade that often carried them in or out of New York harbor.

Large multi-masted schooners were built in New England after 1900. Some had five or six masts and were to a great extent employed in the coal trade. These great schooners for a span of twenty years, more or less, also helped in making up the waterfront panorama at wharves in New York, Brooklyn and New Jersey.

The huge transAtlantic liners that eventually followed in the wake of the wooden paddle wheel vessels were the culmination in making New York the center for passenger travel to and from foreign lands. Docks on the Hudson River in particular, held such ocean crossing giants as the *Leviathan, Olympic, Mauretania, Queen Mary, Queen Elizabeth* and *Normandie.* Today, these docks are sadly quiet much of the time. Harbor traffic still bustles about New York but it too is considerably less than in days gone by.

The tug boat industry expanded rapidly after 1860 and by the 1870's, South Street was a place crowded with the offices of tow boat companies. In its early days, the job of towing vessels, particularly sailing vessels, in from Sandy Hook was often on a first come, first hired basis. Tugs were often owned by their captains and rivalry was fierce among tow boats. Steam was the motivating power of tugs around the turn of the century and the "chug, chug, chug" and sharp "toot toots" from their steam whistles made New York harbor a lively place.

In addition to tugs and their tows of large steamships, sailing ships and many different types of barges, there were the coastal steamers, lighters, ferry boats of different types, excursion boats, sight-seeing boats, fishing boats and other types of small craft. All were busily scurrying about, intent on their own way of earning a living. It made for a lively, often exciting marine pageant for the beholder.

Also, each and every one of the previously mentioned varieties of shipping and craft were vulnerable to accident and mishap. Ever since the days when it was first settled, New Yorkers have borne witness to more than their share of maritime troubles.

The salvage vessel *Relief* underway at high speed on the way to salvage work. Part of her crew are mustered on the stern. The ship was built of steel as a wrecking steamer by Harlan and Howlingsworth at Wilmington, Delaware for the Merritt & Chapman Derrick and Wrecking Company of New York. She was 184 feet long and measured 828 gross tons.

Above: Early in the morning of April 21, 1906 the fishing vessel *Cynthia* went ashore on Romer Shoals. The fishing schooner was returning to New York when the accident happened. The Life Saving crew rowed out to the sunken vessel but found no one on board. **Below:** The schooner was raised by the Merritt & Chapman Wrecking Company on April 22nd and taken to a dry-dock.

The Italian steamer *Vincenzo Bonanno* stranded on Fire Island in dense fog on June 17, 1906. Life Savers from the Point of Woods, Fire Island, Blue Point and Lone Hill stations worked the rescue of the crew. The annual report of the U.S. Life Saving Service for the fiscal year ending June 30, 1906 described the rescue: "Stranded on Fire Island outer bar during dense fog, 2 miles from the former station and 150 yards from the shore, at 8:50 p.m. The keeper of the Point of Woods station, upon discovering her, burned a Coston signal, manned a surfboat and boarded. Upon the request of the master the surfmen then pulled ashore and sent dispatches to the vessel's owners and agent, also to a wrecking company for tugs. As the crew wished to remain on board, the keeper, as a precautionary measure rigged up the breeches-buoy apparatus for landing the crew. At 10:40 a.m. the following day, signals were made on board and two men were brought ashore in the breeches buoy, and 32 landed with the surfboat. All were taken to the station where they were provided with food and shelter, also dry clothing from the stores of the Women's National Relief Association. The wreckers having arrived, the master, agent, and 10 men of the crew were put on board the ship to aid the wreckers in working the pumps. The keeper with his crew, aided by the men from adjoining stations, then stood by the vessel, rendering all assistance possible until the 27th when she was floated and taken to New York."

Early in the evening of June 17, 1906, the Italian steamer *Vincenzo Bonanno* stranded on Fire Island in dense fog, 150 yards from shore. The Life Savers rigged the breeches buoy and stood by until wreckers arrived to save the ship. The vessel was pulled off ten days later by tugs and towed to New York City. *Photo by Anderson, courtesy of Suffolk Marine Museum, West Sayville, New York.*

Above: On October 13, 1906, an autumn fog was the cause of a collision between the Hudson River steamboats *Adirondack* and the *Saratoga*. The *Saratoga* suffered the most damage. The crash tore away the outboard housing of the paddle wheel and caused the port boiler to roll overboard. One man was lost off each vessel. The *Saratoga* sunk near Tarrytown. She was subsequently raised and repaired. She ran on the river until 1910. An old superstition about a steamboat with a name beginning with the letter S came true for the *Saratoga*. The ship was plagued with bad luck. *Photo courtesy of the Steamship Historical Society of America.* **Below:** One man was lost in an unusual accident when the tug *Rescue* came to the aid of the British Steamer *Gowanburn,* stranded on the Long Island coast, twelve miles east of Fire Island light near the Blue Point life-saving station. The vessel came ashore in dense fog in the afternoon of March 13, 1907. The Life Saving crews were notified and brought the beach cart to the scene. The fog was so thick the vessel could not be seen but the fog whistle aboard the ship guided the keeper and he fired his shot line true and it landed aboard. There was no immediate danger and a tug was called. The Merritt & Chapman Wrecking Co. tug *Rescue* arrived on scene and while running a line to the stranded ship, the man running the boat was knocked overboard and lost in the breakers. The ship was floated on March 23rd and towed to New York. *Photo by Anderson, courtesy of the Suffolk Marine Museum, West Sayville, New York.*

Above: The British steamer *Regulus* stranded on Long Island a quarter mile east of the Bellport Life Saving station early in the morning of November 19, 1907. There was little danger but Life Savers boarded her. They brought messages ashore and to the Revenue Cutter Mohawk. The ship was refloated at 7:30 p.m. on the same day. **Below:** On November 30, 1907, the British brigantine *Lady Napier* stranded on the point of Sandy Hook, one half mile north of the Life Saving Station at 7;30 p.m. The Life Savers launched the lifeboat and went to stand by the vessel. At 2:30 a.m. the next morning, the wind and sea increased and the crew of eight were landed. The barkentine was pulled off the beach by wrecking tugs on December 6th and towed to New York. The loss to the cargo was listed as $4,000. *Photos courtesy of the Mystic Seaport, Mystic, CT.*

Above: The two masted schooner *Henry Crocker* went on the rocks just off the bulkhead at Manhattan beach and pounded a hole in her bottom on April 7, 1908. The vessel sank near the beach and her two crewmen jumped overboard. Two men launched a boat from the beach and picked up the crewmen. The schooner was carrying a cargo of crushed stone from Staten Island to Far Rockaway and was caught in the strong winds. **Below:** Shortly after the grounding, the schooner was raised by the Merritt & Chapman Wrecking Company.

Above: The German ship *Peter Rickmers,* bound from Perth Amboy, New Jersey to Rangoon, Burma, was wrecked near Jones Beach, Long Island on April 30, 1908 during thick weather and an easterly gale. The ship was heavily laden with a cargo of 125,000 cases of crude oil and kerosene. Life Savers from the Short Beach Station landed the crew of 33 and wreckers were called to save the vessel. **Below:** A few days later the storm had finished the ship and she broke up. The vessel was a total loss.

Above: On April 9, 1908, at Shinnecock, Long Island, the five masted schooner *George P. Hudson* stranded at 2 a.m. in thick weather one mile east of the Shinnecock Life Saving Station. The vessel was discovered by the east patrol at 4:45 a.m. and life savers set up the breeches buoy. The master landed and made communications with wreckers. That afternoon the tug *I.J. Merritt* arrived and began salvage. The schooner was refloated on April 19th. **Below:** Winslow Homer immortalized the Life Savers with his etching entitled "The Life line" The artist lived on the coast of Maine and no doubt, witnessed several rescues by the Government life-savers.

Above: On the night of June 25, 1908, the American steamer *Chippewa* stranded in dense fog on Long Island about a quarter mile east of the Ditch Plain Life Saving Station. The ship was seen by the Keeper of the station the next morning. He went aboard in a small boat and ferried the captain ashore to report to the owners. Later the Keeper was assisted by the Keeper of the Hither Plain station and volunteers in landing the crew of 28 men and their baggage from the grounded steamer. **Below:** The 2,696 ton vessel was on a voyage from Charleston, South Carolina, to Boston with a general cargo. She was pulled off the beach on August 3rd and towed in for repairs. The Annual Report of the Life Saving Service listed a $59,000 loss in the stranding.

Above: The Boston to New York steamer *H.M. Whitney* ran aground twice in the same year at Hell Gate. On the night of May 23, 1908 the steamer went aground in dense fog on Hog's Back. The vessel remained aground and had to be unloaded before she could be refloated. **Below:** The Merritt & Chapman Wrecking Company removed the cargo of the *Whitney* to barges in order to refloat the ship.

Above: On November 5, 1908, the *H.M. Whitney* again grounded when she swerved to avoid a collision with a barge which had women and children on board. She went on the rocks at Ward's Island and sank by the stern. **Below:** Her crew barely escaped when the vessel went down. She was again salvaged by the Merritt & Chapman Wrecking Company and went back into service.

Above: A tragic accident occurred during a thick fog on November 26, 1908 in the main ship channel, three miles east of Sandy Hook, New Jersey. The White Star freighter *Georgic,* from Liverpool collided with the Panama Railroad Company steamer *Finance.* Four persons lost their lives when the *Finance* went down in fifteen minutes. There were eighty-eight passengers and sixty-seven crewmen on board the vessel when the collision took place. Several of these jumped overboard but were picked up by boats from both steamers. **Below:** The next day, divers were down on the sunken vessel recovering one hundred thousand dollars in gold specie. The boxes of gold were brought back to New York and delivered to a bank for safe keeping. The *Finance* was 2,603 gross tons and was a total loss.

Above: the White Star liner *Republic*, following the collision with the *Florida*. The ship has a large canvas patch on her side covering the hole caused by the accident on January 23, 1909. This vessel was taken in tow by the Revenue Cutter *Gresham* but she sank before they could reach shoal water. All hands aside from the six killed in the initial collision were saved. The *Republic* lies at approximately 40-25.5N, and 69-40.0W. *Photo copied from Harpers Weekly.*
Below: The Italian liner *Florida* lost her bow in the collision, 26 miles southwest of Nantucket Island, off the coast of Massachusetts. This was reported as the first marine disaster where the wireless radio played an important part in the rescue of persons at sea. *Photo courtesy of the Peabody Museum of Salem, Massachusetts.*

Above: The four masted schooner *Miles M. Merry* went aground on Long Island twice in her career, both times in the same spot. On September 10, 1907 she went aground at the Moriches Life Saving Station and was pulled off the next day with no damage. On February 17, 1909 while underway from Boston to Newport News, Virginia, the unfortunate vessel went aground on the same location but with different results. A wrecking crew tried for three weeks to refloat the schooner. They were close to success but on March 15th the vessel caught fire and burned to the waters edge. *Photo courtesy of Capt. W. J. L. Parker, U.S.C.G. [Ret.]* Below: Late at night on February 19, 1909, the freight steamer *John H. Starin* was battling an easterly gale in Long Island Sound. The vessel, built as a revenue cutter in 1865, was carrying a heavy load of freight. Some of the seams opened up and she began to take on water rapidly and the crewmen were working at the pumps steadily. The storm and leaks got worse. The stokers in the engine room were working in water up to their knees. The pilot just spotted the lights on Steeplechase Island breakwater when the steamer lost her way and went on the rocks. Some of the cargo was recovered. The ship was later pulled off and towed to New York City for repairs. *Photo courtesy of the Mariners Museum, Newport News, Virginia.*

Above: The five masted schooner *William C. Carnegie* was wrecked at East Moriches, Long Island on May 1, 1909, in a northeast gale. Twenty-foot seas prevented life savers from effecting a lifeboat rescue from shore. The crew of the schooner cleared a long boat and rowed off shore to await rescue by the cutter *Mohawk*. The vessel was loaded with 4,400 tons of coal. The ship and cargo was a total loss. *Photo courtesy of Capt. W. J. L. Parker, U.S.C.G. [Ret.]* **Below:** The Spanish steamer *Antonio Lopez*, on a voyage from Cadiz, Spain to New York City with a general cargo and 526 passengers went ashore in dense fog a mile south of the Point of Woods Station south of Long Island at 8:45 p.m. on June 9, 1909. Life Savers from the Point of Woods station launched a surf boat and went alongside the steamer. A wrecking tug arrived on scene. The tug removed the passengers and transported them to New York. The vessel was ashore until the 13th when she was refloated.

The steamer *Armitage Brearly* was underway in the Hudson River on the night of December 29, 1909 when she encountered large pieces of ice in the river. The ice pierced the hull of the small steamer and she was assisted to a wharf at Hastings by the steamer *Raleigh*. The *Brearly* sank beside the pier and was later lifted up by the barge Century of New York.

Bk. "FORTUNA", ITALi
ASHORE NEAR SHIP BOTTOM, L.S.S. N.J.
JanY. 18. 1910.

Fog and high winds were blamed for the loss of the Italian bark *Fortuna* on January 18, 1910 near Ship bottom, New Jersey. The vessel stranded near the life saving station. The Life Savers rescued the crew of 13, the master's wife and three children by surfboat. The *Fortuna* was stripped and sold to wreckers. *Photo courtesy of Captain W.J.L. Parker, U.S.C.G., [Ret.]*

Above: The schooner *Daylight* with a cargo of 1,000 tons of coal sank shortly before noon on January 18, 1910 in the Lower Bay after she struck a partially sunken mud dumper scow just outside Sandy Hook, New Jersey. The Captain and crew were saved. Below: The schooner was refloated on March 28th by the Merritt & Chapman Wrecking Company and repaired. She was lost on August 29, 1916 off Palenque, Santo Domingo.

Above: The schooner *J. Henry Edmunds* was anchored off Sandy Hook, New Jersey on the morning of February 2, 1910 when she was run down by a tow of barges and sunk. The crew launched their boat and rowed ashore. The schooner was a total loss. *Photo courtesy of the Mystic Seaport Museum, Mystic, Conn.* **Below:** The Canadian schooner *Garfield White* sprung a leak while on a voyage to Canada with a load of coal on July 5, 1910. The crew fought for twenty-four hours to save their vessel but the schooner leaked faster than they could pump her out. The crewmen abandoned the vessel and made their way ashore in the ship's boat. The *Garfield White* sank off Coney Island. In the photograph, the men in the small boat were tending a diver down working on salvage of the schooner.

Above: The steamer *William Fletcher* which ran between the Battery and Ellis Island hit a spar and sprang a leak. She sank off Governors Island on March 23, 1910. **Below:** Two Merritt & Chapman Company derrick barges lifted the steamer off the bottom.

Above: The tug *Reliable* caught fire off New Rochelle on April 19, 1910 and burned to the waterline. **Below:** The United States Monitor *Puritan* sank off Gray Island on November 18, 1910.

Above: The fishing schooner *Robert C. Harris* struck a submerged object and cut a hole in her hull on August 5, 1910 off the coast of Sandy Hook, New Jersey. The Gloucester fisherman had 3,500 pounds of bluefish in her hold. Life Savers from the Monmouth Beach station pulled alongside in a surfboat and took the eight man crew off the vessel and landed them ashore. **Below:** The schooner grounded near the station. She was pulled off the next day and towed to New York by a wrecking tug. While on shore, beach visitors climbed aboard the schooner and pilfered part of the catch of fish.

Chapter Six

In the New York Evening Post, Albany Gazette, there appeared in September, 1807, the following advertisement:

```
          The North River Steamboat will leave Pauler's Hook Ferry
     (foot of Cortland Street) on Friday the 4th of September at 9 in the
     morning, and arrive at Albany on Saturday at 9 in the evening.
     Provisions, good berths and accommodations are provided. The
     charge for each passenger is as follows:

     To Newburg          dols   3            time        14 hours

     Poughkeepsie               4                        17

     Esopus                     4-1/2                     20

     Hudson                     5                         30

     Albany                     7                         36

     For places apply to William Vandercoort, No. 48 Courtland street on
     the corner of Greenwich Street. Way passengers to Tarry Town, &c
     &c will apply to the captain on board.
```

This advertisement for Fulton's new steamboat *Clermont*, ushered in a new era in coastal passenger travel. Others soon attempted to duplicate Fulton's success. The Fulton & Livingston Line fought doggedly for seventeen years to hold on to their monopoly of the steamboat passenger trade on the Hudson River. In 1824, however, their lucrative monopoly was successfully challenged by others.

Certainly, many of the early steamboats were crude affairs as far as engines, accommodations and safety were concerned. With their tall funnels belching black smoke, thrashing paddle wheels and hot furnaces, they were looked upon with a certain amount of anxiety by the traveling public. Occasionally the boiler on one of these early vessel would explode with disastrous results to anyone nearby. Many regarded them as "infernal machines" and wouldn't go on board for any reason, preferring the slower sailing packets instead.

One innovating company tried to circumvent fear of the steamers by towing passenger barges that were fitted out with all of the passenger comforts found on the steamers but lacking an engine or sails. Unfortunately the barges and their tow boats were slower than the unencumbered steamers, often arriving three or more hours after the latter.

After the Erie Canal opened in 1825, the traffic on the Hudson increased dramatically. Along with the many tows of barges carrying cargoes of all sorts, the increasing numbers of passenger steamers had to watch out for the ever present schooners and sloops that were always operating on the river. Hudson river schooners and sloops were generally of a type so peculiar to

111

Above: Several vessels including the Norwegian bark *Ingrid* were badly damaged in an explosion at the pier in Jersey City, New Jersey on February 1, 1911. The New York Maritime Register reported that the bark had her decks, masts and upper works badly wrecked in the explosion. **Below:** A freight vessel, the Katherine W., was blown to pieces and the power boat Whistler was sunk. Seven barges and a steam hoister were damaged. When the Whistler was raised, a portion of the boat was intact and five cases of dynamite were found on deck.

the area that they almost became a class unto themselves. Wide of beam, shallow of draft and fitted with centerboards, they were also lofty and could carry a fairly large press of sail. Many were most attractive from a nautical point of view. As the canal boats evolved, they also became distinctive in appearance. They had to be narrow enough to negotiate the many locks found in the Erie Canal and also burdensome enough to carry a paying cargo.

Families, some of reportedly rough repute, generally lived on board the canal boats. Their quarters were located in a house, or cabin, usually near the stern of the boat. Some of the fancier canal boats even had stern windows, or lights, cut into their transom. The bows on most of the barges were generally very round or bluff, coming to a point at the stem. Cargo was loaded and unloaded through a continuous system of hatches that ran from a few feet aft of the bow to a point just ahead of the aft living quarters.

While traveling along the canal the barges were towed by mules which usually were quartered on board when their services weren't required. When going up or down the Hudson, the barges were often "bunched up" and pulled by tow boats. There were also canal boats that were designed just to carry passengers. While some were fitted out with elegant accommodations, others carried only the most basic elements required by the trade. In addition to the canal boats, other types of barges were increasingly seen on the river. Some of these were box barges which carried coal or other bulk cargoes, while others were of a scow design and could transport very heavy deck loads.

With all of the preceding vessels of various sorts busily scurrying about serving the river ports between Albany, Troy and New York, increased caution in navigation was needed to avoid unwanted mishaps. Collision and strandings were not uncommon.

By 1826, there were sixteen coastal steamboats in service. By 1840, there were around one hundred that were puffing their way along coastal routes. The monopoly held by the sailing packets on protected inland routes was slowly but surely coming to a close. The sailing packets held out on routes going to less important ports for the better part of the 1800's, but as the steamers improved both in safety and in scheduled arrivals, the wind driven vessels lost trade.

As their engines increased in power and efficiency, the size of the steamboats increased as well. The steamer *Alida*, which was built by George B. Collyer in New York in 1847, was 265 feet long. On one occasion she went from New York to Albany, making one stop on the way, in under eight hours time. This was a far cry from the sailing packets which under some circumstances took almost a week.

The *Alida* was purchased by Commodore Alfred Van Santvoored in November, 1855. Around 1863, the Commodore, in partnership with others, started the famous Day line operating on the Hudson. The first two boats owned by the company were the *Daniel Drew*, built in 1860 and the *Armenia*, built in 1847. Both were built by Collyer in New York. The company changed its name to Hudson River Day Line in 1899.

Although there were many competing companies operating on the Hudson, certainly the Hudson River Day Line became one of the best known. The company operated thirteen different vessels over the long course of its history, finally going out of business in 1948.

In 1949, the Hudson River Boat Company, Inc., was able to change its name to Hudson River Day Line, Inc., and for a time operated three of the old Hudson River Day Line steamers, namely the *Robert Fulton*, the *Alexander Hamilton* and the *Peter Stuyvesant*. The vessels were no longer used for the long runs to Albany, but were often chartered for excursion purposes. The line finally went out of business during the 1960's, after being bought out by the Circle Line of New York.

Long before the advent of railroads, there were steamboats operating on Long Island Sound. The first steamboat trip from New York to New Haven, Connecticut, occurred on March 25, 1815. The steamer *Fulton*, under command of Captain E.S. Bunker and carrying 30 passengers, made the passage in little over eleven hours.

In 1816, the new steamboat *Connecticut* arrived at Norwich, Connecticut for the first time. Regular operations to and from New York were started in 1817. Along with the *Fulton*, both vessels made regular trips with New London and New Haven as additional ports of call.

Prior to 1825, other steamboats were forbidden to operate between Connecticut ports and the port of New York due to the monopoly held by the Fulton & Livingston Company. Passengers traveling to New York from Bridgeport, for example, had to be landed at Byrams's Cove, near Port Chester, New York and proceed from there to New York by stage coach.

Above: When barges broke loose from their tug in a storm it was difficult to predict where they would end up. Most were wrecked on the beach but the Powelton Barge #10 was in the Housatonic River at the time, ten miles from Long Island Sound. When the tide dropped, she was left high and dry, posing a difficult salvage job for the Merritt & Chapman Wrecking Company. **Below:** An odd accident occurred at Weehawken, New Jersey on June 11, 1912 when the Cleary Brothers Scow turned over atop a Canal Barge at the railroad coal docks and created more problems for salvage men.

114

After the Fulton monopoly was knocked out, there were many steamboat services opened up into a number of ports located along the Connecticut shoreline. Due to the nasty nature of weather conditions frequently experienced on the sound, the steamers that operated there were often built to different specifications than were river steamers. Seaworthiness was a very important part of Long Island Sound steamboat design. Sails were usually carried on most of the early steamboats. As time went on towards the mid 1800's, the sound steamers gradually got larger and the sails began to disappear.

During the mid 1820's, service between New York and Providence, Rhode Island was inaugurated and by 1827, four steamboats were making regular runs between the two ports. In 1845, railroad service between Fall River and Boston was completed. And the next year, Colonel Thomas Borden and his brother organized the Bay State Steamboat Company, a company that was to become famous and widely known as the Fall River Line.

In 1846, the company purchased the two largest coastal steamboats of their day; the *Massachusetts* and the *Bay State.* The *Bay State* was 317 feet in length and made the initial run on the Fall River Line on May 19, 1847. She was eventually lengthened to measure 352 feet. This vessel made a trip between New York and Fall River, in 1857, that took only eight hours and forty-two minutes. She continued to work for the line for 17 years and was then sold to be converted to a coal barge.

In 1863, the Bay State Steamboat Company sold the Fall River Line to the Boston, Newport & New York Steamboat Company, which made Newport its terminal instead of Fall River. In 1869, the Boston Newport & New York Steamboat Company was taken over by a rival company, the Bristol Line and the two companies then became the Narragansett Steamship Company with the main eastern terminal returned to Fall River.

In 1872, the Fall River line was completely reorganized under the control of the Old Colony Railroad. The new company was called the Old Colony Steamboat Company. In 1893, the Fall River Line came under the control of the New Haven Railroad Company, which by 1899 was the mentor of five Long Island Sound steamship lines. The railroad was to control seven lines eventually.

For nearly ninety-one years, the Fall River Line remained in active service and then following a union sit-down strike, a judge's ruling on July 27, 1937, put an end to the line's operations. When the strikers decided to get back up from their sit-down strike, they found that they no longer had jobs.

All during its years of operation, the Fall River Line had stayed with the use of paddle wheel passenger steamboats. As the line prospered, their passenger vessel got larger in size until in 1908, the huge *Commonwealth* was launched for them by William Cramp & Sons at Philadelphia, Pennsylvania. She was 456 feet in length and the biggest inland passenger steamboat ever built.

Other Fall River steamboats that were well known were the *Providence, Priscilla, Plymouth, Puritan* and *Pilgrim,* all very large vessels whose names began with the letter P. They also owned many other steamers including a number of freight boats that ran between New York and Fall River.

Their huge passenger steamers were fitted out with the best accommodations that were then available. Their cuisine was excellent. Described by many as "floating palaces", they indeed looked the part as they made their stately trips through Long Island Sound. As a boy, I can vividly remember the sparkling brilliance of their lights as they steamed by my home town off of Rye, New York, during many a calm summer evening.

Although their safety record was a relatively good one, the Fall River Line did have some casualties. Nine passengers died as a result of a boiler explosion on the *Empire State* in July, 1856. One passenger was killed when the *City of Taunton* collided with the *Plymouth* in March, 1903 Their vessels suffered from a number of strandings but in all cases were saved and returned to work. The *Bristol* was destroyed by fire in 1888 and the wooden upper works of the *Plymouth* were burned off down to her steel hull in March, 1906, but she was rebuilt. Other companies operating steamboats on the sound were no as lucky. Over the many years of steamboat operation in Long Island Sound, the number of vessels and lives lost created a list whose reading, was rather grim.

At 4 a.m. on April 6, 1911, the 10,881 ton North German Lloyd steamer *Prinzess Irene* stranded during a thick fog on the outer bar a mile east of the Long Hill Life Saving Station on Long Island. The Life Savers went aboard but the vessel was resting easy and in no danger. There were, however, 1,725 passengers on board.

The Prinzess Irene

The 1911 Annual Report of the U.S. Life Saving Service carried the following: April 6, 1911 -"The largest vessel to suffer casualty within the scope of the service operations during the year was the 10,881-ton North German Lloyd steamer *Prinzess Irene.* The disaster in question occurred while she was en route from Mediterranean ports to New York with 1,725 passengers, a crew of 263 and carrying a large general cargo. She stranded during a thick fog at 4 a.m. on the outer bar a mile east of the Lone Hill station, coast of Long Island. She was discovered about daylight by the east patrol of the station mentioned and within a short time the life- saving crew from that place were abreast of her where they were later joined by the Blue Point and Point of woods life-saving crews. The Lone Hill crew launched their surfboat immediately upon their arrival and boarded the vessel where they remained at the master's request, until the following morning to quiet the fears of the passengers. Soon after they went on board, they signaled to their comrades on the beach messages to be forwarded to the vessel's owners and to underwriters, revenue cutters and wreckers. In response to the calls, the revenue cutters *Seneca* and *Mohawk* and the wrecking steamer *Relief* arrived at 3 p.m. and arrangements were made for salving the vessel. As she appeared to be in no immediate danger of breaking up, the Blue Point crew returned to their station on the evening of the 6th, while the Point of Woods crew stood by on the beach all night ready to render any assistance that might be necessary. On the morning of the 7th, the Blue Point crew returned to the steamer and arrangements were made for placing the passengers aboard the steamer *Prince Frederick,* which was then on its way from New York to the scene of the stranding. In the meantime, a line was run from the vessel to the shore and the beach apparatus placed in position ready for use should it be found necessary to resort to that method of landing those on board. The transfer of the passengers to the *Prince Frederick* began at 2 p.m., and was concluded in three hours without accident. Three boats manned by life savers, five from revenue cutters and two from wrecking steamers participating in the work. While the transfer was in progress, anchors were planted and lines run from the vessel to the revenue cutters and to several large wrecking steamers. On the next high tide an attempt was made to haul her off. Similarly unsuccessful efforts were made on succeeding high tides. On the 8th, part of the vessel's cargo was transferred to lighters and taken to New York. The steamer was floated on the 9th and proceeded to New York, convoyed by a wrecking fleet. This disaster involved loss to the owners of approximately $70,000, counting only damage to vessel and cargo."

On the next day, the Long Hill Life Savers were assisted by others from the Blue Point and Point of Woods stations. They transferred all of the passengers to the liner *Prince Frederick* in three hours. Some of the cargo was lightered off the stranded liner and she was pulled free on April 9th and towed to New York City. *Photos by Anderson, courtesy of the Suffolk Marine Museum, West Sayville, N.Y.*

Above: On the night of May 20, 1911, the steamer *Central Hudson* grounded off Stony Point in the Hudson River. She was refloated and went aground a second time on the 22nd off West Point. Cause of the grounding was dense fog in both accidents. Three days later, wreckers floated her off with the aid of pontoons and she was towed to Brooklyn for repairs. **Below:** The steamer *Penobscot* went aground on the night of June 11, 1911 in the Hudson River during an extra high tide. The ship was stuck at Stockport Flats for 26 days. It was necessary to dredge a channel around her. With the help of several steam derricks and a dozen tugboats the vessel was refloated. In 1918, the old hull was converted to a five-masted schooner named the *Mohawk*. She sailed for less than a year and went missing.

On October 7, 1911, the three-masted schooner *Frederick Roessner* ran up on the breakwater near Peacock Point in Matinicock, Long Island. A storm with high winds and rain followed by a thick fog caused the grounding. The rocks stove a hole in the bottom of the vessel. The schooner had a cargo of stone which was unloaded. She was hauled off on the 16th and towed to New York for repairs. *Photo courtesy of Capt. W.J.L. Parker, U.S.C.G. [Ret.]*

The same storm and fog that grounded the *Frederick Roessner* was the cause of the Canadian schooner *Coral Leaf* to go aground, a quarter of a mile away. The schooner with her cargo of spiles lay on a sandy beach and was soon pulled off by salvagers.

Above: The tugboat *Transfer No. 4* sank near Pier 18 on January 15, 1912. The Fall River liner *Providence* is in the background. **Below:** The tug was raised by the wrecking barge MONARCH, only to sink again a year later at Pier 11 in the Hudson River.

The fruit steamer *Jose* was loading case oil for Jamaica on March 13, 1912 when a keg of oil fell into the hold and burst, starting a fire that could not be controlled. The vessel was towed away from the pier and sank in the river about 300 feet from shore. Hundreds of spectators came to the waterfront to watch the blazing ship. The Merritt & Chapman Wrecking Company raised the ship in July and towed her to a dry-dock. In the photograph above, the Merritt & Chapman Wrecking Company is using floats to raise the vessel. After she was raised off the bottom she was towed to shallow water in the photo below.

Above: The Fruit steamer *Jose* was towed with men at her helm to shallow water where she was pumped out and refloated. **Below:** After refloating, the steamer was hauled to a shipyard for repairs.

The Merchants and Miners Line steamer *Ontario,* while on a voyage from Baltimore to Boston, caught fire in number one hold while off Montauk Point, Long Island on April 8, 1912. The fire was out of control and the heat drove the crew out of the pilot house. They lashed the wheel and the vessel was driven aground near Dead Man's Bend. The 32 passengers were transferred by one of the ship's boats and the Life Saving Crew to the tug *Tasco,* which landed them at New London. Three Revenue cutters, the *Acushnet, Mohawk* and *Seneca* battled the flames but the fire in bales of cotton burned on for two weeks before it was extinguished. The vessel was refloated on April 29th and towed to New London.

Details given in the annual report of the Life Saving Service for the fiscal year ending June 30, 1912 outline the services of the Crew of the Watch Hill, Rhode Island, life saving station at the wreck of the burning steamer *Ontario* on the morning of April 8, 1912. Keeper Walter H. Davis reported as follows: "I launched the power lifeboat and set out in search of the steamer. Four members of my crew accompanied me. We left our station at 3:15 a.m. with a dory in tow. As we were unable to sight the steamer after leaving Watch Hill reef, we steered for Montauk Point. As the tide was flood and running against the wind, the trip was exceedingly rough. The seas broke over us almost continuously.

"When we were within about 4 miles of Montauk Point, rockets were seen to shoot up some distance westward of the Point which told us that the vessel was on the south side of Long Island. As we hauled out to southward the vessel came plainly into view at the place where her captain had beached her under full steam.

"Ours was the first boat of any description to reach the disabled steamer. The life-savers from Ditch Plain had, however, arrived on the beach abreast of her somewhat ahead of us and rigged up the breeches buoy apparatus. Running our boat in alongside and going aboard, we discovered that the whipline operating the buoy had snarled and that the buoy itself was hung up 100 feet or more out from the port forerigging, to which the hawser supporting the buoy had been made fast. I at once climbed into the rigging, overhauled the whip, cut out the knot, spliced the line with the aid of two of the ship's crew and then signaled for those on shore to haul away. The buoy was thereupon run out to the steamer. The distance between the vessel and the shore was about 700 feet and the operations from the shore were conducted from the crest of a bank 80 or more feet high.

"After the tide had made ebb and the seas somewhat subsided, Capt. Parsons of the Hither Plain station arrived with his power surfboat towing an open surfboat and all hands began the work of transferring the passengers and their baggage to the wrecking tug *Tasco*. I and my crew carried the first load, consisting of 12 women in one of the *Ontario's* boats. Capt. Parsons and his crew also transferred a load in his surfboat and the ship's second officer concluded the work of transfer in another of the steamer's boats, the 32 passengers and their baggage being taken off by 9:30 a.m.

"While the transfer of passengers and their effects was going on the Ditch Plain life-saving crew came aboard in the breeches buoy and joined the vessel's crew in fighting the fire. The conditions were such that the hose could be manned for only a few minutes at a time, the steam and smoke being so stifling that those engaged at the four different nozzles through which water was being played into the vessel's hold were compelled to work in relays.

"We cut holes through the deck, broke windows and resorted to every conceivable means to reach the fire which was then confined in the lower hold and difficult of access. So intense was the heat that the nozzles of the hose would occasionally be burned off.

"About noon, the wrecking tug *Harriet* arrived with a lighter. The latter vessel was run in on the starboard side of the steamer abreast of the midship gangway and the transfer of the *Ontario's* freight began. While cargo was being placed on the lighter, the life-savers engaged in lightening the steamer by throwing overboard hundreds of barrels of vegetable truck, bales of burning cotton, etc. The lighter finished loading about 6 p.m., and later in the evening the revenue cutter *Acushnet,* which had reached the scene about noon, was hauled alongside in a position favorable for pouring water into the vessel. Three streams were thrown from the cutter throughout the night. At the request of the captain of the *Ontario* we remained on the vessel overnight and assisted in fighting the fire. At 5 a.m. of the 9th, there being nothing further we could do, and all hands being greatly exhausted, we returned to our stations."

The vessel was hauled off by the Merritt & Chapman Wrecking Company but there was a $395,000 loss divided between the ship and cargo.

On the night of April 14, 1912, the 66,000 ton White Star liner *Titanic,* on her maiden voyage to New York City struck an iceberg four hundred miles south of Newfoundland and foundered, taking over 1,500 persons to their deaths. The *Titanic* carried lifeboats for only half of the passengers and her loss is considered the greatest maritime tragedy in the history of ocean travel. *Photo courtesy of the Titanic Historical Society, Inc., Indian Orchard, Massachusetts.* The Grave of the *Titanic* was originally positioned at approximately 41-46N, 50-14W.

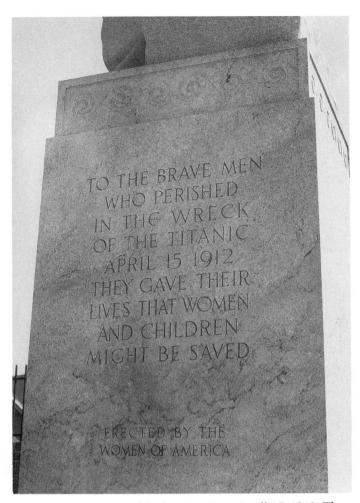

The women of America erected a monument to the men who went down with the *Titanic* on April 15, 1912. The memorial is in Washing Channel Park in the southwest portion of the Nation's capital city. The base of the statue has an inscription which carries the thoughts of those who erected it.

On April 14, 1912, the greatest tragedy in modern maritime history occurred when the steamer *Titanic* struck an iceberg, 400 miles southeast of Newfoundland and sank two hours later to the ocean floor, two miles below the surface. No other maritime disaster in history has so captured the headlines and continues to do so to the present day. Her story is well known; the brand new White Star liner was steaming along in the North Atlantic at 22 knots on her maiden voyage to the United States. Despite repeated warnings, just before midnight, the ship hit a huge iceberg. Her location was flashed by radio to all the ships at sea to come to her aid. The coordinates were 41-46 north and 50-14 west. The iceberg had ruptured the side of the ship underwater and she was sinking. The vessel was equipped with fourteen lifeboats, two cutters and four collapsible boats with a capacity of 1,178 persons, or, a little more than half of the 2,206 persons aboard the liner. There were 1,503 persons lost. Only 706 people survived in the lifeboats. The popular illusion that the ship was unsinkable persisted in the minds of many passengers until most of the boats had left and it was too late when the terrible truth was realized. There were eleven millionaires aboard the *Titanic* along with the cream of European and American society, including John Jacob Astor. These men went down with the ship. Since the disaster, many books have been written about that memorable night. Hollywood has created movies about the *Titanic* and interested marine buffs formed a society devoted to the memory of the ship. Following the sinking, the International Ice Patrol was established in the north Atlantic. The patrols continue to this day and each nation using the northern steamer routes pays its share of the expense. Every year the anniversary is marked by a Coast Guard plane dropping a ceremonial wreath near the spot where the ship went down. In September, 1985, the wreckage of the *Titanic* was located by an expedition from the Woods Hole Oceanographic Institution. The hull was found by two remote control submersibles at a depth of approximately 13,000 feet.

Above: The Pilot schooner *Ambrose Snow No.2,* was rammed and sunk by the Clyde Liner *SS Delaware* in Lower Bay on May 13, 1912. The schooner sunk almost immediately after the collision. The crew left the vessel in the yawl boat and went aboard the *Delaware.* There were no injuries to any of the crewmen. **Below:** The schooner was salvaged by the derrick MONARCH of the Merritt & Chapman Wrecking Company on May 24th.

Above: The sightseeing yacht *Osprey* rammed a heavy barge near east 97th street in the East River on July 11, 1912. The yacht had seventy-five passengers aboard when the accident occurred. The collision took place near Hell Gate and several boats nearby came to the aid of the passenger laden steamer. Everyone was saved and the captain maneuvered his craft to let her sink near the shoreline. **Below:** It seems that whenever a maritime disaster of any sort happens near the shore it attracts large crowds of onlookers. The *Osprey* sank close to shore. The vessel was later salvaged.

Above: The wrecking tug *Hustler* recovered a truck from the bottom of the North River on July 10, 1912. Accidents like this were common in the days of open ferry boats and less than dependable brakes. One can surmise that the truck was moving down the ferry and its brakes failed. It most likely went over the open end of the ferry and right to the bottom. There was probably little loss, in that the accident happened in July, so the driver could jump clear and swim to safety. The truck was predictably a total loss after being dunked in salt water and was only removed to clear the ferry slip from an underwater obstruction. **Below:** Two thousand members of New York's Hudson County Democratic Club boarded the steamer *Persus* on the evening of September 11, 1912 for an outing. The steamboat accidentally ran up on a reef opposite the College Point ferryhouse and punched a hole in her hull below the waterline. She began to sink but, quick action by two passing tugboats saved the day. The tugs pushed the *Persus* across to the ferry slip and her sister ship, the *Sirius*, was nearby to aid in removing the Democrats. Everyone got off safely. The vessel was later salvaged. *Photo courtesy of the Mystic Seaport Museum, Mystic, Connecticut.*

Above: On October 10, 1912, a boiler explosion on the oil tanker *Dunholme* caused a conflagration at the Standard Oil Company oil docks on Constable Hook in Bayonne, New Jersey. Flames from the fully laden tanker spread quickly to four other ships at the docks. Two of the ships were saved but two others, the *Concordia* and the *Hohenzollern* were lost to the fire. The flames created what was referred to as a brilliant spectacle, but it cost the lives of three men. **Below:** The *Concordia* was towed out into the stream to burn off the cargo. The ship was a total loss.

Above: The wooden steamboat *Cimbria*, out of New Brunswick for South Brooklyn, with a cargo of copper wire, was in collision with the lighter SAFETY, one hundred feet from shore opposite Bayonne, N.J. in the evening of December 9, 1912. The bow was badly stove in and the vessel started to settle to the bottom. The captain ran his vessel towards shore and grounded her twenty-five feet from the shoreline. **Below:** The vessel was later raised and repaired in a dry-dock.

The schooner *L. Herbert Taft* while on a voyage from New York to Havana, Cuba, went aground on December 19, 1912 near Swash Channel in the Lower Bay. The crew was taken off by the Life Savers from the Sandy Hook Station. Efforts were made to refloat the vessel but salvagers could not save her. She was stripped. The hull and cargo were declared a total loss.

"S.S. TURRIALBA"
Ashore NORTH BRIGATINE SHOAL JERSEY BEACH
DEC. 24, 1912.

Above: The British steamer *Turrialba* came ashore near Little Egg Harbor shoals off New Jersey on December 24, 1912, during a thick snowstorm. Life Savers removed the passengers the next morning. **Below:** The vessel was refloated three days later by the Merritt & Chapman Wrecking Company and towed to New York. Part of her cargo was thrown overboard to lighten her for floating. The ship lost her rudder in the accident.

"S.S. TURRIALBA"
ASHORE NORTH BRIGATINE SHOAL JERSEY BEACH
DEC. 24, 1912

Above: The Norwegian Steamship *Nicholas Cuneo* came ashore at Fire Island on February 5, 1913 in stormy weather. Wreckers were called in and jettisoned part of her cargo. The ship was refloated on February 11th and towed to Robins Dry-dock in Brooklyn, N.Y. for repairs. **Below:** The barkentine *Antioch,* from Savannah for New York, stranded about 500 yards from shore near the Squan Beach Life Saving station in thick weather on March 26, 1913. The Life Savers rigged the breeches buoy but had to use a team of horses to keep the hawser taut because of the force of the current. The rescue took twelve hours to complete. Life Savers landed ten men from the grounded vessel. Keeper Longstreet of the Squan Beach station broke four hawsers in completing the rescue.

Above: The fishing vessel *Norseman* came ashore on Sandy Hook, New Jersey on May 25, 1913. The 90 ton schooner returning from a fishing trip got lost in the fog and she lay over on her starboard side when the tide went down. The crew of 17 men were taken off by the Life Saving crew, in the boat rowing alongside. The vessel was pulled off a few days later and towed to New York. *Photo courtesy of Richard M. Boonisar, Norwell, Mass.* **Below:** The German steamer *Mohawk* suffered an explosion in one of her fuel tanks on June 27, 1913 while at anchor off Tompkinsville. Several men were killed and a dozen injured when the blaze broke out. The ship sunk by the stern as tugboats pumped water in her to extinguish the fire. On July 1st, the ship was pumped out and taken to a shipyard for survey.

Above: Abandoned hulls are part of shipping. The photograph shows an old paddlewheel ferryboat burned out and sunk near Shooters Island. The damage is extensive and the rest of the vessel probably rotted out. **Below:** Steamships are built with a twenty year life expectancy so they seldom grow old. When they outlive their usefulness they are consigned to the breakers yards. The paddlewheel steamers (L. to R.) *Princeton, Newark & Naiad* are old. They lie and wait to be dismantled. *Photo courtesy of Mystic Seaport.*

Above: This is the Meseck Line steamer *Wauketa* with her Playland banner running from the bow. The line ran daily trips to the Playland Park in Rye from Battery Park in lower Manhattan. The run to the park took about two hours. **Below:** The crew of the *Wauketa* during lifeboat drill. The boats were swung out and lowered a few feet. Sometimes they would put them in the water and row around but this was only on rare occasions.

Chapter Seven

One of the memories that remain vivid from my younger days were the excursion steamers that came to Playland Park. The *Americana, Wauketa, Westchester* and the big *Richard Peck,* were all Meseck Line steamboats when I was a boy.

Playland was located at Rye, New York on Long Island Sound and during the 1930's, many people came to the park by boat. The Meseck Line, whose offices were at 17 Battery Place, in New York City, ran daily trips that started from Exchange Place at Jersey City. It took a half an hour to get from Exchange Place to Battery Park on Lower Manhattan. From there, the boats left promptly at 9:45 in the morning bound for Playland. From the park, some of the boats then went on to Bridgeport, Connecticut. The round trip fare to Playland was $ 1.75 for adults and 75 cents for children. On Sundays and holidays, the fare increased by 25 cents.

The trip to the park took about two hours. The passengers could then go ashore and spend a few hours and a few dollars on some of the rides and amusements found at the park. They were then returned to New York on an evening boat. There was dining on board and dancing to a live orchestra. On weekends and holidays the boats were usually filled to capacity.

After prohibition had been repealed in the early 1930's, draft beer was sold on many of the excursion steamers. It was customarily dispensed in large paper containers that often blew about the boat when emptied. There was good reason for the paper containers. A beer bottle in the wrong hands could be a lethal weapon.

Frequently on many of the chartered trips to the park, "hard liquor" was brought on board in picnic baskets and other covered containers. Often some of the parties held on deck became quite raucous and what with people bunched together in such close quarters it was not uncommon for tempers to flare, fists to fly and fights to start. Many an outing was marred by a few individuals who had one too many and "couldn't hold their liquor". The crews on the steamers generally had among their members, those who were big enough to handle most of the unruly drunks. However, occasionally things did get out of hand.

My father was an official at the park and I remember one time when one of the captains on the Meseck Line told him of a case that really got out of control. The incident didn't happen on one of the Meseck boats so I guess the captain felt safe in disclosing it. The particulars of the story occurred aboard a rival steamboat when a boatload of excursionists began battling one another and then turned on the boat crew. The trouble really started after a large percentage of the passengers had shown up for their outing already feeling the effects of too many drinks.

After the boat left her berth, the drinking continued and before very long a real brawl broke out. The crew of the steamer tried to halt the battle in their usual way but the passengers began using some of the folding deck chairs as assault weapons and the crew was forced to retreat to the ship's fire hoses. The fire hoses were then brought into play and water was sprayed on the howling passengers in hopes that it might cool some of the hot tempers. Unfortunately, it had just the opposite effect.

As if gasoline had been poured on a fire, the brawl burst forth into a real riot, and with drawn knives, some of the passengers went after the crew. The crew quickly dispersed behind locked doors. The passengers then ran amuck. Windows were smashed and furniture ripped up and thrown about. Deck chairs along with any loose gear were tossed overboard. Some of the steamer's officers armed themselves and then barricaded the doors inside the pilot house. Then they headed for the nearest port. After the boat was successfully placed alongside a pier, police armed with "billy clubs" jumped on board the badly damaged steamer. They put an end to the rampage and to the excursion. Some of the worst offenders spent the rest of their holiday in the local lock-up.

Above: The *Christian D. Emson* ran on a rock in Pelham Bay on May 16, 1911. The schooner was fully loaded and extensively damaged by the rock. She was pulled off by the Merritt & Chapman Wrecking Company. The *Emson* was built in 1866 in Keyport, New Jersey. **Below:** The *John P. Wilson* sank beside a wharf at City Island on July 5, 1913. The vessel had left New York for a trip to Stamford, Connecticut, when a leak developed and the flooding could not be controlled. There were fifty passengers aboard and her Captain decided to head into the island to avoid a tragedy. Everyone got off safely and the steamer sunk minutes after arriving at the landing. She was raised on the 9th by the Merritt & Chapman Wrecking company and was towed to New York.

There were, of course, times when the Meseck Line landed its share of characters, some of whom staggered ashore in a loud and advanced state of intoxication. However, there was always a park policeman on hand at the gangplank to escort those who offended society off to the jail within the park. There they were left to sober up for the return trip to the Battery. Happily, most of the travelers were well behaved and enjoyed the boat ride and the visit to the park.

My family often made a weekend trip to the Battery and back just for the fun of the boat ride. It was a marvelous way to spend a Saturday or a Sunday. The sights along the way were always of great interest and the many harbor craft that we passed always enhanced the trip. Passing through the East River and Hell Gate was never a dull experience. We would usually remain on board at the Battery after the boat was unloaded. After the boat was reloaded, we would head back for Playland. Mother always packed a great lunch so no one wanted for food.

One return trip I remember quite well. During our passage to New York, a northeast breeze had built up. By the time we were making the return trip, it was blowing quite hard. If I remember correctly, we were on board the *Wauketa*, which was the smallest of the steamboats managed by the Meseck Line. Before we had gone very far into the reaches of Long Island Sound, we were surrounded by whitecaps and the *Wauketa* was jumping around in a much more lively fashion than was usual. Many of the passengers who had been happily talking and laughing began to grow quiet. Seasickness soon began to rear its ugly head.

As seasick people often do, some of them tried to lay down. This only made their condition worse. On our crowded steamboat, there weren't really many places available for people to lay down. Some of the more advanced cases simply sprawled out on the upper decks. The seas that were washing aboard into the lower deck areas made laying down in that part of the boat pretty much out of the question. Crew members with buckets and mops tried their best to clean the upper decks, but the decks soon became slippery again after each cleaning. Passengers who were not violently ill did their best to grab onto anything that was securely fastened to the boat. With white knuckles, they clung there in one spot until the laboring steamer finally arrived off Playland pier.

The pier at Playland was partially protected by breakwaters built out on each side and in spite of the choppy seas, the captain of the *Wauketa* did a fine job in docking his vessel. My brother Bill and I thought that the whole boat ride was just great. There were though, of the passengers who disembarked that day, some who were shorn of their rosy glow. They looked a bit more grey-green in appearance. A few were heard to say flatly that they planned to take some other form of transportation back to the city. There were also some who were too weak to walk off the boat and they had to be helped ashore by sympathetic crew members or members of the park's personnel.

Seasickness and excessive drinking not withstanding, the business of running excursion boats was indeed a paying proposition fifty or more years ago. Going for picnics and outings on a steamboat was something that was eagerly looked forward to by many people from the middle of the 1800's right up to the mid 1900's. Around the turn of the century, there were a large number of popular places to visit by way of excursion boats. Poughkeepsie and Bear Mountain were frequent destinations located on the Hudson River. During the late 1800's, John H. Starin built up Glen Island off New Rochelle. This resulted in a good sized fleet of excursion boats that brought passengers up Long Island Sound to this popular playground. Glen Island finally closed as a resort in 1916.

Above: The United Fruit steamship *Metapan* sunk at her pier on August 9, 1913 after a seacock broke and flooded the ship with water. At the time it was feared that the ship would turn over and sink beside the dock but she settled with only a slight list. **Below:** The crew were removed and the wrecking tugs of the Merritt & Chapman Wrecking Company were called in. The *Commissioner* and the *I. J. Merritt* pumped out the water and returned the steamer to a floating condition on August 13th.

There were several fleets of steamboats that brought happy patrons from the city to Coney Island, located near the western end of Long Island. The Iron Steamboat Company had seven paddle wheel vessels that operated for a period of over forty years between the Battery and Coney Island. When the line finally went out of business the entire fleet was sold in February, 1933, for $15,050. The depression of the late 1920's and early 30's had a terminating effect on all sorts of businesses.

Rockaway Beach, Long Island, became a popular summertime destination for many sweltering city people. In the 1870's, Mr. R. Cornell White ran five steamboats to Rockaway. The Knickerbocker Steamboat Company ran there with the big steamers *Columbia* and the *Grand Republic* during the late 1870's. The ill-fated *General Slocum* replaced the *Columbia* in 1888. Fire tragically ended the career of the *General Slocum* when she burned in the East River on June 14, 1904, with the loss of 1,031 lives. Most of the victims were German-American school children who, along with their mothers, were heading for a picnic at Locust Grove, not far from Throg's Neck in the Bronx. The *Grand Republic* also went up in smoke when on April 25, 1924, she and the steamers *Nassau* and *Highlander* burned at their Hudson River piers while being made ready to operate for the coming summer season.

Many New Yorkers headed for the sandy beaches located along the shores of New Jersey. One of the easiest ways to get to New Jersey was by boat. *Point Comfort* and *Keyport,* a couple of old time side wheelers from the Nantucket run ended their days running between the Battery and Keansburg, New Jersey.

In addition to the excursion boats there were literally dozens of commuter steamboats carrying passengers back and forth during the late 1800's and early 1900's. There was even a passenger boat commuting service between Wall Street and Harlem back in the mid 1800's. While Manhattan, Staten Island New Jersey and Long Island may seem close by today's standards, getting from one of these places to another was best accomplished by boat not too many years ago.

Photographs taken back in the 1880's and 1890's, show New York's waterfront packed to the point of bulging. Many of the smaller passenger steamboats tried to travel on fixed schedules as best that conditions would allow. People often commuted on a regular basis. During winter freeze-ups, ice clogged waters presented a real problem. Trips across the Hudson, East River and Upper Bay were often cancelled or held up for hours. On a year round basis, crowded harbor traffic sometimes led to collisions that badly damaged or sunk the commuters' means of transportation.

Ferryboat service carrying passengers, wagons, horses, trucks and cars increased steadily following the Civil War. By 1929, there were 44 separate ferryboat routes operating in and around the waters of New York City. There were even specialized ferries that carried only railroad cars back and forth from Manhattan, New Jersey and Long Island. By the mid 1970's, the only floating shuttle service left open to the general public was the famous Staten Island Ferry. The Circle Line still operates sight-seeing trips around Manhattan and special boats carry passengers to the Statue of Liberty, but the old days of crowded commuter travel by water, in most cases, are long gone.

After 1957, the Meseck Line sold its interests to the Wilson Line, which continued in operation to Playland Park for another year. In 1961, the Wilson Line withdrew its New York services. Many of their vessels were either retired out of service or sold for other use.

While most of the excursion lines did well, there were times when some of their steamboats had moments of trial and tribulation. Fire and collision were problems that many faced and in some cases resulted in heavy loss. Many of the old boats were built with wooden superstructures which were most always painted with white lead paint. Once a fire got well under way on vessels of this type it inevitably meant the loss of the steamboat. It was appalling as to how fast these fires could race from bow to stern.

After the passenger carrying sound steamer *Maine* went on the rocks near Execution Lighthouse in February, 1920, it proved to be beyond salvage. It was decided to burn off her wooden upper superstructure to aid in the demolition of the big steamer. A fire was therefore started in the forward part of the old boat. According to one of the wrecking crew members, who was there at the time, it took only eight minutes before the entire 300 feet of wooden superstructure was burning fiercely. One need not wonder why lives were lost when such vessels caught fire while under way against any kind of a breeze.

Above: The New York to Albany steamer *Mohawk* struck an embankment off Hyde Park on the night of September 28, 1913. The vessel suffered a large hole in her bow and other unlisted damages. She was refloated by the Merritt & Chapman Wrecking Company and brought to New York for repairs. **Below:** Fire at sea is one of the sailors worst enemy. The British steamship *Volturno* was abandoned on fire on October 10, 1913 in the mid-Atlantic. The ship was on a voyage from Rotterdam for New York via Halifax. Several ships provided assistance in the storm tossed waters of the North Atlantic. There were 657 persons on board of which all but 131 were accounted for after the survivors were brought ashore. The rescue vessels stayed in the vicinity and launched several lifeboats to save as many passengers as possible. The ship was a total loss and the British government dispatched a cruiser to destroy the wreck.

In the days before Coast Guard regulations for passenger carrying vessels were enacted, many boats were crammed full to the point where sitting room was sometimes unavailable. Lifeboats, fire fighting equipment and life saving equipment were either in short supply or in poor repair. This was not the case in all boats, but in many there were serious shortcomings. Eventually all passenger carrying vessels were limited to the number of passengers that they were allowed to carry. Adequate life preservers and lifeboats were required for all hands. In addition, fire and lifeboat drills had to be carried out at regular intervals during the season of their operation by the crews on board the steamboats.

I can remember some of the drills that were conducted on several of the steamboats that arrived at Playland. Normally, the drills were done after the passengers had disembarked at the park. Alarm bells were sounded, hoses brought forth and water sprayed out over the harbor area. The lifeboats were swung out on their davits and lowered a few feet. Most of the time they were not put into the water. I also recall a couple of occasions when the lifeboats were put into the water and some of the steamboat crews tried their competence at rowing. They didn't do to well. An old timer who was watching growled:

"Good Lord, they caught more crabs than you'd find in a fish market!"

Today, much of the excursion boats are only memories that are occasionally talked about by the "older generation." Most of the time, the memories are good ones. You have to go a long way back to talk about the really bad ones.

The four masted schooner *Marjory Brown* sank in the Atlantic on October 20, 1913 off the coast of Long Island at Lat. 40-35N.,Long. 71-32W. This dramatic photograph was taken by a crewman of the German passenger steamer *Berlin* as a boat from that vessel took the crew off the sinking schooner. The boat is just astern of the *Marjory Brown*.

Above: On December 8, 1913, the steamer *Zulia* was loading cargo at a pier in Brooklyn when a heavy steel shaft broke through its case and fell into the hold damaging the vessel and causing a bad leak. The ship was towed to the mud flats off Red Hook, New Jersey, where she sank with her decks awash. **Below:** The bridge was the only section of the ship above water. The salvagers had to work fast before winter weather arrived.

Above: The Merritt & Chapman Wrecking company spent a few days to move wrecking steamers into place before raising the steamer *Zulia*. Divers had to be sent down to seal the hull in order to raise the vessel. **Below:** Workmen in small boats alongside the sunken steamer sunk off Conover Street, Brooklyn on December 8, 1913.

Above: The tug *W.A. Sherman* sank at the foot of South Street in New York in 1914. The small tug was later raised and repaired. **Below:** A large railroad barge sank on October 24, 1914. The freight cars sank along with the barge. The salvage of this barge required a couple weeks work by the Merritt & Chapman Derrick & Wrecking Company.

Above: The excursion steamboat *Mediator* sank at Newark, New Jersey in 1915 alongside her pier. The vessel was raised by the Merritt & Chapman Wrecking Company. **Below:** The oyster boat *Waldron B. Oyster* went up on Throgs Neck in a storm on February 5, 1915. The rocks damaged her bottom somewhat but she was pulled off and repaired.

Above: The work of rescue attracted a large crowd on February 7, 1914, when the British steamer *Queen Louise* stranded near Squan Beach, New Jersey in dense fog. There is a movie camera located behind the breeches buoy crotch. Perhaps the rescue appeared in the newsreels. *Photo courtesy of the Mariners Museum, Newport News, Virginia.* **Below:** The Life Savers stood by the steamer until February 9th, when the apparatus was removed. The vessel was refloated on the 10th and proceeded to New York under her own power.

Above: On April 15, 1914, while anchored in gale winds off the Monmouth Beach Life Saving Station, the schooner *Charles K. Buckley* began to drag her anchors and was ultimately dashed on the beach with the loss of seven persons. Only one man survived. Life Savers fired shot lines over the vessel but only one man was still alive on board. He managed to get the line and tie it around himself and was pulled through the surf and wreckage to shore. The large crowd gathered on shore to watch the operations, hindered the Life Saving crew but, at that point, almost everyone had already been lost. The schooner washed ashore a couple of days later and was a total loss. *Photo courtesy of Capt. W.J.L. Parker, U.S.C.G. [Ret.]* **Below:** The *Iroquois*, ran aground on the Hudson River in a night fog at Cementon, New York on April 20, 1914. The *C.W. Morse* tied on to the grounded vessel and tried to pull her off but the hawser broke. The steamer was stuck on the bank for a week before she was pulled off by the wrecking steamer *Champion*. *Photo courtesy of Allie Ryan.*

Above: The cattle boat *General McCallum* sank at 14th street in Hoboken, New Jersey on October 2, 1915. The livestock aboard the vessel was lost and she was raised by the Merritt & Chapman Wrecking Company on October 4th. **Below:** The steamer *Lowell* sank at her pier at 26th street on the East River on May 7, 1916. The Merritt & Chapman Wrecking Company raised the vessel and she went back into service.

Above: The sightseeing boat *Tourist* ran into the stern of a long string of barges and canal boats in the Hudson River near Yonkers on June 20, 1914. The accident killed one of the men and caused the loss of one barge. The *Tourist* sank on a bar near the shore. The vessel was later raised by the Merritt & Chapman Wrecking company and repaired.
Below: On July 10, 1914, the Norwegian steamer *Manchioneal* ran into the pilot boat *New Jersey* off Sandy Hook, New Jersey in dense fog. The collision sank the pilot boat about 200 feet from the entrance to the Ambrose Channel. All that could be seen of her were two masts rising out of water. The crew was rescued by the crew of the *Manchioneal* and crewmen from the U.S. Dredge RARITAN which was nearby. In the photograph, the salvage vessel *Commissioner* had divers down the the sunken vessel. The vessel broke in two pieces and was abandoned.

Above: In the Ambrose Channel outside New York, on October 15, 1914, a dense fog rolled in and blanketed the waterway. The United Fruit steamer *Metapan* entering port from South America was struck near the bow by the freighter *Iowan*. **Below:** The captain of the *Metapan* piloted his ship into shoal water and rammed her into a shoal to keep her from sinking. The 76 passengers and 92 crewmen were all saved. The vessel was later raised and repaired.

Above: The Canadian schooner *Annie Marcia* grounded on the southern end of Hart's Island at 7:30 p.m. on November 15, 1914, during a southeast storm. The vessel was loaded with lath from Newcastle, New Brunswick, for New York City, and was later pulled off the beach. **Below:** The Norwegian steamer *Preston* left New York city on the night of January 28, 1915, bound for Sweden with a half million dollar cargo of cotton and lumber. A fire was discovered in the hold and she was anchored near the Statue of Liberty. The New York fireboats *William J. Gaynor* and the *New Yorker* assisted in flooding the hold. The *Preston* sunk at anchor. The ship was pumped out on February 2nd and towed to Arnott's Stores in Brooklyn to discharge the cargo. A diver's examination of the bottom of the ship found no damage.

Above: The British bark *Hugomont* stranded on Fire Island on February 6, 1915. The ship was bound from London to New York with a cargo of chalk. The Coast Guard set up the breeches buoy and removed the crew of 20. Seven members remained on board. Soon after, wreckers arrived on the scene. *Photo courtesy of Capt. W.J.L. Parker, U.S.C.G. [Ret.]* **Below:** After unloading a third of the cargo, they refloated the bark on the 19th and towed her to New York City. *Photo by Anderson, courtesy of the Suffolk Marine Museum, West Sayville, Long Island.* Note: On January 29, 1915, the Revenue Cutter Service and the Life Saving Service merged by Presidential order into one unit and called the U.S. Coast Guard.

Above: The British bark *Invermay*, while in ballast, came ashore early in the morning of April 12, 1915 on the beach at Mantoloking, New Jersey. The bark was driven off course by a storm and the Captain could not get his bearings. The vessel was pulled off the next day and towed to New York to take on a cargo of wheat for the British Army. *Photo courtesy of Captain W.J.L. Parker, U.S.C.G., [Ret.]* **Below:** The New York, New Haven and Hartford Railroad tug *Transfer No. 6* was sunk in an odd accident on April 27, 1915. The tug had a barge in tow and a hawser broke. The big barge dropped astern and stove a hole in the side of the *Transfer No. 6*. Captain Leach attempted to steam away from the side of the barge but inrushing water sank the tug. The crew scrambled aboard a float and were picked up by another tug. The *Transfer No. 6* was later raised by the Merritt & Chapman Wrecking Company.

Above: The Long Island Sound steamer *Isabel* sunk at Shippan Point just south of Stamford, Connecticut in Long Island Sound on September 28, 1915. Some of her cargo is stacked on deck as another steamer pulled alongside. Most of the cargo was recovered but the steamer was a total loss. **Below:** The Portuguese bark *Pero d'Alemquer* stranded at Mantoloking, New Jersey on December 18, 1915 with a load of corkwood and 23 people on board. The Coast Guardsmen landed the crew and then assisted wreckers and Revenue Cutters in refloating the ship on December 23rd. The 15,000 ton vessel left the United States in January and went missing with all hands.

Above: On April 20, 1916, the freight steamer *Lansing* was in a collision with the tug *Transfer No. 15* off the Battery. The *Lansing* had her bow stove in. She sunk at the foot of 27th Street in Brooklyn. The Merritt & Chapman Wrecking Company raised the ship on May 10th. She was towed to dry-dock for repairs. **Below:** The British ship *Artensis* went ashore at Seaside Park, New Jersey at 1 a.m. on June 8, 1916 in heavy fog. Coast Guardsmen landed the crew of 19 in the breeches buoy.

The *Artensis* lay in six feet of water just off shore and was not damaged. The 1,709 ton ship was refloated at 10 p.m. on June 18th by the Merritt & Chapman Wrecking Company and was towed to New York.

Above: On July 22, 1916, the sidewheel steamer *Keyport* was rammed on the port side by the steam lighter SANTOS and sunk off the Battery. Before she settled, she was shoved broadside against a sea wall where her passengers leaped ashore. **Below:** Salvage was attempted as cranes from the Merritt & Chapman Wrecking Company removed the wreck but the vessel was a total loss.

Ship "Clan Galbraith".
Near Shinnecock, Long Island.
July 22, 1916.

Above: The Norwegian bark *Clan Galbraith* in heavy weather and dense fog ran aground near Shinnecock Inlet, Long Island on July 22, 1916. The four masted steel bark was in ballast from England to the United States to take on a cargo of oil. **Below:** The 2,168 ton square rigged vessel lay on the sands for about two weeks. Tugs from New York floated the ship on August 4th. She was later sunk by a German U-boat in World War II.

162

Above: The steamer *Marion* sank off South Norwalk, Connecticut on March 10, 1916. She was raised and repaired by the Merritt & Chapman Wrecking Company. **Below:** The United States Transport *Sumner,* bound for New York from Colon, Panama, went aground in dense fog near Barnegat, New Jersey on December 11, 1916. The steamer had 800 tons of scrap iron on her forward hold and she was hard on the bar. The 232 passengers went down over rope ladders into Coast Guard motor lifeboats and were brought ashore. The ship broke up on the bar and was a total loss.

Above: Holiday excursions were the ultimate in personal entertainment during the halcyon days of the 19th century. New York steamboats carried thousands of passengers to and from the parks and amusement areas. The lithograph depicts steamers in Rockaway Inlet and was published by Harpers Weekly in September, 1878. The artist was not far wrong from the truth about the heavy traffic in the waterways. **Below:** Many steamers caught fire and sank in New York waters. This unidentified steamer sank with smoke still coming out of her hold.

Chapter Eight

After the installation of the steam engine on boats, New York harbor was witness to an increase in the operation of machine driven watercraft of varying size and types. The hustle and bustle of harbor vessels busily engaged in their work added much to the color and character of this famous port. Following the turn of the century, a visitor to New York's waterfront was confronted with dozens of small harbor craft that were chugging their way through often choppy waters, frequently tooting at one another and occasionally running into trouble.

There were lighters and barges of different kinds seemingly everywhere. Also the numbers of tugboats seemed to be without end. A visitor might suspect that tugboats had always been there as a part of the waterfront panorama. In fact, towboating in New York harbor does go back a long way. The first regular towboat service was established there by the old side wheeler *Rufus W. King* in 1828. The first towboat line was established in the New York area by Isaac Newton of Renssalaer, New York.

All of the very early towboats were paddle wheel steamers. The venerable *Norwich* was undoubtedly the longest lasting of these old veterans. She was built as a passenger vessel in 1836 and for five years carried people to and from New York and Norwich, Connecticut. After her Long Island Sound passenger carrying days were ended she was brought to the Hudson River. Here, after some alterations, she spent most of the rest of her career in use as a towboat. She was finally listed as abandoned by her owners in the 1924 issue of the U.S. List of Merchant Vessels. The first propeller driven tugboat to operate in New York waters was the *Sampson*. This vessel was built in the Cramp yard in Philadelphia, Pennsylvania in 1850, at a cost of $4,500.

From the mid to late 1800's, there were many tugboat companies formed in and around New York. One of the most successful was the company formed by Michael Moran in 1860. Moran was a young Irish immigrant who advanced himself from working as a mule driver on the Erie Canal in the 1850's to becoming an agent and owner of tugboats in New York City. He first got started in the business when he purchased a half interest in the harbor tugboat *Ida Miller*. He then opened up an office at 14 South Street in New York on November 10, 1860, where he conducted business as a towboat agent.-

By the mid 1880's, there were over 150 tugs operating around New York harbor and Michael Moran held an interest in ten of them. The vast majority of the harbor tugs were owned at least in part, by their captains and often the engineer held shares as well. Their business was conducted on a strictly cash and carry basis. Frequently, a good deal of haggling ensued before a deal was struck and any towing undertaken. It was a rough and ready crowd who ran the tugboats in New York and occasionally battles between rival crews erupted. When it came to deciding who was going to tow a particular vessel, sometimes the crew with the heavier fists got the job. Price, however, was usually the deciding factor.

As time went on, many of the Moran tugboats were given family names. The first tugboat in the fleet to receive the name of a family member was the *Maggie Moran,* built in 1881 and named after Moran's first wife. This vessel coast $6,000 and was driven by a propeller. In 1892, Michael Moran bought the old side wheeler *Belle* for $7,000. She had a cross head engine and had been built in 1837 as an excursion steamer. She was rebuilt in 1851 as a towing vessel and in appearance looked very much like the old *Norwich*. After only five years service she was condemned and had to be broken up.

Above: Tugboats played an important role in the traffic in New York waters. These nine tugs all have the American flag flying and were no doubt getting ready for a parade up the Hudson. **Below:** The largest tugboat company in New York was undoubtedly the Moran Establishment. Many of their boats were named after a member of the family. This one is the *M. Moran.* The photograph was made in the summer of 1916.

During the 1880's, the pride of the Moran fleet was the tug *F.W. Vosburg.* This 90 foot vessel was built in 1883 at Athens, New York, by Wentworth Allen. She could steam along at twelve knots and would often outrace any of her rivals, getting to an inbound ship before others could begin the haggle about who was to pass the hawser. For twelve years she was much in demand, not only as a towboat, but for quick trips to harbor disasters.

On March 10, 1895, at 2:30 a.m., the *F.W. Vosburg* struck on Romer Shoal during a snow storm. She sank almost immediately. Her crew had just barely enough time to scramble aboard the dump scow they had been towing out to sea. The Sandy Hook Life Saving Service crew discovered the wreck at daybreak and promptly started a three mile row against heavy wind and seas. Another tug reached the wreck before the Life Savers and removed Captain Frank Cutler and his tired, half frozen crew of six men. The Life Saving Crew cut the scow loose from the sunken tug, fearing the floating vessel was likely to do damage to the Romer Shoal beacon. The scow was then taken in tow by the tug *Ramsay,* and brought in under the lee of Sandy Hook. Unfortunately, the swift *F.W. Vosburg* was a total loss. Such losses were not uncommon, however, in most cases the situation was reversed with the losses occurring at the other end of the tow line.

The Moran Towing and Transportation Company grew steadily as the years progressed into the 1900's. By 1910, the company was grossing nearly $800,000. By the time World War Two was upon us, the company was grossing ten times the former figure and they owned fifty tugs. The Moran tugs were generally painted with bright red deck and pilot houses. Each tug had a black painted funnel with a white letter M affixed near the middle of the stack. They were quite distinctive when seen from any distance and became well known in all of the east and Gulf coast shipping areas. The company is still one of the largest of its type in operation today.

In addition to the Moran company there were other towing organizations that got an early start in the business. Some of these were the Cornell Towing Co., E.E. Barrett & Co., McAllister Brothers, Shamrock Towing Co., Fred B. Dalzell, the John E. Moor Co., the Russell Brothers Towing Co., and the Gamecock Line.

Lewis and Edward Luckenbach were pioneers in the business of ocean towing and by the 1880's, vessels from their fleet of ocean going tugs and schooner barges were often seen passing through New York waters. Lewis Luckenbach died in 1906, and his son Edgar took over control of the business. Ocean going tugs grew to a very large size, some being in excess of one hundred and thirty feet in length. They had to be very powerful to maintain way against strong weather conditions while towing sometimes as many as six schooner barges loaded with coal. Many of these coal barges were destined for New York or the industrial ports of New England. More than a few of these laboring long tows ran into serious difficulties along the way. The coasts of New Jersey and Long Island were littered with the remains of schooner barges that came to grief during spells of bad weather. Some of the tugs doing the towing were lost as well.

During the 1920's, the numbers of long tows began to decrease. Coal was gradually being replaced by petroleum fuels and the roar of diesel engines began to supplant the more humble chug, chug, of the old steam engines. Many of the older steam tugs were converted to diesel power during the mid and late 1920's. The conversion was often not difficult, but with the loss of their tall funnels, the appearance of many tugs was drastically changed.

Tugboats had the job of helping large ocean going vessels into their berths on the Hudson and East Rivers. While the sailing ships of early days had to be towed in past Sandy Hook, later day liners could steam all the way to the upper bay under their own power. However, getting alongside and securely fastened to their piers was another matter. Even though periods of slack tide were chosen for docking time, there were usually currents and eddies flowing in both rivers that could cause problems. Strong winds also added to the difficulties. In the winter time when ice often clogged the harbor, it frequently took as many as ten tugs to get a huge liner safely into its berth.

In addition to their everyday roles of towing and pushing, tugs were frequently sent upon errands of mercy. Moran company tugs were often involved in efforts to help others who were in trouble. On June 30, 1900, a terrible fire broke out at the North German Lloyd docks in Hoboken, New Jersey. The fire apparently started in some bales of cotton and quickly spread. The wind was blowing nearly forty miles per hour and the blaze became intense, jumping from pier to pier. Many barrels of whiskey piled on the docks awaiting shipment were surrounded by flames. When the whiskey exploded, the fire ran rampant. To many observers, it looked like the whole Hoboken waterfront was going up in smoke.

Above: The tug *Catherine Moran* sank beside a barge in 1919. Unattended vessels sometimes ended up on the bottom for short periods of time. Sometimes the crew would tie up, visit the local pub for a quick brew and when they returned, the boat was on the bottom. **Below:** The steamer *Manchuria* was heavily damaged in a collision with the U.S. Monitor *Amphitrite* in the narrows on June 13, 1917. The monitor was equipped with a ram which did substantial underwater damage to the steamer. The *Manchuria* was sunk off Staten Island at Stapleton. The cargo was removed by the Merritt & Chapman Wrecking Company prior to raising her for repairs.

There were four big liners berthed at the docks, namely; the *Bremen,* The *Kaiser Wilhelm der Grosse,* the *Main* and the *Saale.* These vessels were too large to be quickly moved and were soon ablaze. Many tugs were dispatched to assist in any way possible. All day long and through the night, tugs, fireboats and firemen fought the fire. The *Main, Saale* and *Bremen* were destroyed. Many other vessels were also damaged or lost. A large part of the waterfront with its warehouses and piers went up in flames. The damage in dollars amounted to $10,000,000 and there were 326 lives lost.

There were several accusations made, that some of the tugboat captains brutally ignored people struggling in the water. They said they were left to drown when they informed the tugboat that they couldn't pay for their rescue. Also another tugboat was accused of cowardice for not trying to tow the blazing liner *Saale* away from the dock. Many of the tugboat companies were incensed by these accusations. After a meeting of the tugboat groups at the produce exchange building, a reward of $1,000 was offered to anyone who could prove that any captain or employee on a tug was guilty of misconduct. The Hoboken fire was one of the worst disasters of this type since the Staten Island ferry *Westfield* blew up in 1871, while in her slip at Whithall Street. This tragedy took close to 100 lives.

Tugs were often sent out on rescue missions. On December 25, 1904, the British tramp steamer *Drumelzier* left New York and headed out to sea into the teeth of a howling northeast snow storm. Shortly thereafter while fighting the huge seas and blinding snow, she ran hard aground on Fire Island Bar. Distress signals were immediately set as the storm was intensifying and huge breaking seas were pounding the grounded vessel. The steamer soon began to show signs that she might break up. On the morning of December 26, a patrolman from the Oak Island Station saw the wreck. He quickly notified his station and the Fire Island Station. Both crews launched surf boats to go to the aid of the grounded steamer. Unfortunately, the rescue efforts of the lifesavers were rejected. Captain Nicholson, aboard the *Drumelzier* thought that the storm would abate. He was wrong. The gale only grew worse.

By late afternoon, a wrecking vessel, the *I.J. Merritt,* belonging to the Merritt & Chapman Wrecking company was standing by, but could not get close enough to the wreck to render any help. After sixty hours or more had passed, those on the doomed ship began to realize that she wasn't going to stand up to the crushing surf much longer. However, they had no way to abandon ship. Fortunately for the shipwrecked crew, a Moran tugboat, the *Catherine Moran* had gone to the Sandy Hook Life Saving Station to assist the lifesavers in rendering help. The crew from the Sandy Hook station boarded their little craft and then with the unsinkable lifeboat in tow of the tug, headed out into the storm wracked night. It was a wild ride for both boats.

The next morning, after being towed to a point near the wrecked vessel, the life savers cut themselves loose from the tug. After pounding off the ice that had formed, the life savers set reefed sails on their careening craft and started working their way in toward where the lurching steamer lay grounded. They were able to sail in under the lee of the liner and took off sixteen of her tired and frightened crew members. Through superb seamanship on the part of both lifesavers and those on the tugboat, the rescued seamen were transferred to the tug and then with the lifeboat in tow they all headed back for Sandy Hook. From Sandy Hook, the *Catherine Moran* then brought the weary survivors back to New York.

Meanwhile, a lifeboat from the *I.J. Merritt* was able to get near the *Drumelzier* but couldn't get back to the wrecking vessel. The lifeboat was forced to head in for the beach and after passing through the breaking surf was safely landed on shore. Following this, the surfboat crews from the Oak Island and Fire Island stations were able to launch their surf boats. After much effort they were able to get next to the wrecked steamer and remove the rest of the crew. The *Drumelzier* became a total loss and was smashed to pieces in the pounding surf.

As some of the Drumelzier's crew were bound to say: "You couldn't expect anything but bad luck when you start out on a voyage on Christmas day."

Above: The tug *Edwin Terry* sank in the Hudson River on August 28, 1917. The photograph was taken during salvage efforts as cables are rigged in preparation to setting the vessel upright. **Below:** The tugboat *James T. McGuire* ran aground at Sandy Hook, New Jersey in the late fall of 1917 and was pulled off by the Merritt & Chapman Wrecking Company.

Above: In the early 1920's, the facade of the T.A. Scott Wrecking Company shipyard storehouse in New London, Connecticut displayed quarterboards from numerous vessels wrecked up and down the coast of Long Island Sound. The grim list resembled an obituary, perhaps as a warning to mariners. Below: An unidentified steamship capsized beside a pier, somewhere in New York with a salvage vessel alongside and sightseers out in rowboats looking on at the operations. This was probably taken in the summer when the weather was warm and the seas calm.

Above: The four masted schooner *Dustin G. Cressy* was rammed by the steamer *Valeria* in New York's lower bay on February 19, 1917. She was struck on the starboard side about midships and she rolled over on her beam ends. **Below:** A Merritt & Chapman Wrecking Company derrick began to work on the vessel a few days later.

The Dustin G. Cressy

The four masted schooner *Dustin G. Cressy* while on a voyage from Jamaica to New York was nearly cut in two by the steamer *Valeria* about 4:30 p.m. on February 19, 1917. The collision occurred in the narrows and the sailing vessel sank almost at once. The *Valeria* had just left New York on a voyage to Liverpool while the *Dustin G. Cressy* was making a tack out of the channel towards the anchorage off Staten Island.

The sailing vessel was only five years old at the time and had a cargo of dyewood aboard. She went on her beam ends and sank in the channel. The schooner's crew had no time to launch their yawl boat or put on life jackets. The accident was witnessed by small craft in the area. One of these, the boat Staten Islander, hurried to the scene and rescued the crew of the *Cressy*.

When the *Cressy* sank in sixty feet of water, she had all her sails set. This hampered salvage efforts but the barge Century managed to pick her up and take her to dry-dock. The schooner was repaired eventually and went back to sea. The *Valeria*, with ten thousand tons of war munitions, anchored in the bay to survey the damage to her bow plates before she proceeded to sea. The *Dustin G. Cressy* was preparing to lay over in the anchorage area before proceeding to Stamford, Connecticut. Her cargo was consigned to a chemical company there. The 182' long schooner was built in Bath, Maine in 1912. She measured 862 gross tons. The Cunard freighter was libeled in the mishap. The rules of the road in 1917 gave a sailing vessel the right of way over steam powered ships.

Above: The tug *John E. McAllister* sank in the East River near Blackwell's Island on the night of July 7, 1917 after striking an uncharted hidden rock. The tug was towing a barge and was bound for South Amboy, New Jersey at the time. The eight persons on board the tug jumped aboard the barge as the tug went down. The *John E. McAllister* was raised the next day by the Merritt & Chapman Wrecking Company and went back into service. **Below:** On July 30, 1917, the steamship *Saratoga* was in collision with the steamer *Panama*. The *Saratoga* was badly damaged. She was taken to a dry-dock for repairs. Before she could be dry-docked her stern settled to the bottom. She was later refloated and repaired.

Above: The barge *New Jersey* went ashore in Hell Gate early in October, 1917, and stove a hole in her hull on a large rock. The vessel was unloaded and raised by the Merritt & Chapman Wrecking Company. It was off Pier 44 in the East River where the photograph was made, on October 15th, after being raised and towed in. There is a wrecking crane barge alongside and the *New Jersey* is down deep in the stern. **Below:** On December 13, 1917, the steamer *Minnesota* was bound from New York to Boston when she hit a submerged rock while passing through Hell Gate. The accident created a large hole in the hull below the waterline and the vessel was beached at Lawrence Point in the Bronx where she sank by the stern in fifteen feet of water. The *Minnesota* was subsequently raised by the Merritt & Chapman Wrecking Company and towed to a dry-dock for repairs.

Above: The steamer *H.F. Dimock* was heading up the East River when she grounded near the abutment of the Williamsburg Bridge on December 26, 1917. The vessel sank but was raised on January 4, 1918 and brought to the pier. The *Dimock* had a checkered career at sea and had many accidents. **Below:** The barge CENTURY of New York displayed her operator's talent when she picked up the fishing vessel *Seneca* beside a pier. The salvage barges were run with steam and could pick up small vessels with ease.

Above: The steamer *Rhode Island* was built in 1882 and ran for several years in Long Island Sound. The hull was later abandoned and she was rebuilt as a coal barge. When war broke out in 1914, she was converted to a six-masted schooner and sold to The Contenental Trading Company of New York. The new owners renamed the vessel *Dovrefjeld.* The schooner sunk at Stapleton, Staten Island on August 14, 1917 while on her way to Europe with a cargo of steel ingots and coke. She was raised on the Aug. 17th. Later she was lost off Cape Hatteras, North Carolina in 1919. **Below:** The steamship *Susquehanna* went aground on March 7, 1918 near Barnegat on the New Jersey shore in thick weather. Coast Guard men landed the crew of 38 with the breeches buoy and assisted in unloading the cargo of china clay. The steamer was pulled off on March 14th by the Merritt & Chapman Wrecking Company and towed to New York.

     The 2,599 ton steamer *Kershaw* ran aground off shore from Ocean Avenue in the town of East Hampton, Long Island in dense fog on March 12, 1918. The Coast Guard could not use surfboats to rescue those on board because of the high seas running at the time. They rigged the breeches bouy from the beach to save the crew. The buoy set up required a heavy line to run the buoy back and forth. This was called the hawser. The control lines to transport the buoy was called the whip line. A unique set-up evolved when automobiles were attached to the whip line and their power was used to run the breeches buoy back and forth to the ship. The hawser was run over the top of a building in order to keep the persons coming ashore from getting soaked.

     Conflicting reports given at the time, instilled some mystery in the salvage efforts. Included in the cargo were 17,000 cases of whiskey. The New York Maritime Register reported that: "Little hope is held for saving the cargo of liquor and tobacco of the steamer *Kershaw*. The vessel was fast breaking up last night. Capt. James McDorman in command of the vessel was the last man brought ashore of the 71 passengers and crew yesterday." A report in the Annual report of the U.S. Coast Guard states: "Vessel was floated April 2nd by wreckers with a loss of $560,000 from a full valuation of $1,050,000 of the vessel and cargo". Most of the $560,000 loss was probably in liquid form and spirited away during the undercover of darkness.

The steamer *St. Paul* was being transferred from a dry-dock at the Erie Basin in Brooklyn on April 25, 1918, to her berth at Pier 61, in the North River. As she came alongside the pier, she suddenly listed to port, turned over on her side and sank in the mud. The cause of the accident was thought to be an ash port left open. Three men died in the accident. It took the Merritt & Chapman Wrecking Company five months to refloat the huge vessel using an elaborate set up of A frames and winches to set her on an even keel. She was towed back to the dry-dock in Brooklyn and overhauled. *Photo courtesy of the Mariners Museum, Newport News, Virginia.*

Above: The U.S.S. *San Diego*, CA-6. The photograph was taken in January, 1915. The name of the vessel had been changed on September 1, 1914 from the U.S.S. *California* **Below:** On July 19, 1918, the *U.S.S. San Diego,* an armored cruiser, struck a mine, ten miles southeast of Fire Island and sank in twenty minutes. The explosion ruptured the steel hull of the cruiser below the water line and killed three men instantly. Three other men were lost when the ship sank but there were 1,183 survivors. A few boats and liferafts were launched from the cruiser before she sank but there were over a thousand men in the water. These men were picked up by the steamers *Malden, Bussan* and *E.P. Jones.* The Navy sent mine sweepers to the area and three contact mines were destroyed. *Photos courtesy of the U.S. Naval Historical Center. Lower photo from a painting by Francis Muller, 1920.*

Above: The steamer *Huttonwood* was being loaded with drums of benzol on August 7, 1918 when a drum broke through the straps of a sling. It dropped into the hold and burst. The fumes came in contact with flames and an explosion followed. **Below:** The tug *G.H. Dalzell* towed the *Huttonwood* into mid stream where she sank under the streams of fireboats. The Merritt & Chapman Wrecking Company went to work on her and salvaged the remainder of the cargo.

Above: The U.S. tanker *Frederick R. Kellogg* was torpedoed and partially sunk by the German Submarine U-117 on the night of August 13, 1918, thirty miles south of Ambrose Channel lightship off Long Island. Seven of her 42 man crew were reported missing. The ship was salvaged and continued to sail. *Photo courtesy of U.S. Naval Historical Center, Washington, D.C.* **Below:** At 10 a.m. on August 14, 1918, the German submarine U-117 fired a warning shot across the bow of the five masted schooner *Dorothy B. Barrett* off New Jersey. The vessel was abandoned by her crew who left her in a motorboat. The submarine then shelled the schooner until it sank. Surface craft were called in but the undersea raider escaped. The crew landed at Cape May.

182

Above: The British steamship *City of Lahore* caught fire in her hold on November 26, 1918 while alongside the pier at 46th street in the North River. The ship was loaded with paraffin and other inflammable cargo. **Below:** Fire fighters filled the vessel with water in order to save the hull and she sank beside the pier. The *City of Lahore* was salvaged by the Merritt & Chapman Wrecking Company.

Above: The troopship *America* sank at pier 3 at Hoboken, New Jersey on October 14, 1918. Cause of the sinking was blamed on neglect of her crew when they left coal ports open. **Below:** She sank in 40 feet of water and the Merritt & Chapman Wrecking Company were called in to refloat the vessel.

Above: The norwegian steamer *Nils* sank on the West Banks on December 15, 1918 after striking the submerged wreck of the steamer *Port Phillip* in the Lower Bay and was run into shallow water. **Below:** The vessel lay on the bar until January 18th, 1919 when the Merritt & Chapman Wrecking Company refloated her. The *Nils* was towed into New York for repairs.

Above: The United States transport *Sixaola* was deliberately sunk at pier 9 in Hoboken, New Jersey on February 23, 1919. The steamer was loaded with hundreds of tons of provisions for the American forces in France when she caught fire in the hold. Feeding the flames were lard, butter and beef valued at three million dollars. The cargo was a total loss and two men were lost fighting the fire. The vessel lay on the bottom until June when she was raised by the Merritt & Chapman Wrecking Company and towed to a dry-dock. The *Sixaola* was built in 1911 and was of 5,017 gross tons. **Below:** Another view of the harbor taken from atop a tall building at a busy waterway. Several tugboats, ferries, barges, a steamer and a two masted schooner are visible. Patches of snow appear here and there and smoke coming up would set the time in winter.

Above: On February 28, 1919, the steamer *Aquitania* coming up the harbor collided with the British freighter *Lord Dufferin*. Damage to the freighter was extensive and resulted in lengthy lawsuits. Below: The ship lost about forty feet of her stern. The hull was immediately beached. She was refloated on March 21st.

Above: On March 17, 1919, the tug *William A. Jamison* was sunk near pier 15 in the East River following a collision with the steamboat *Lexington* of the Colonial Line. The crew was rescued by another tug and brought ashore. A dense fog which hung over the city, caused numerous accidents with other tugs and ferry boats. A number of persons were injured in the several collisions in New York waters but none seriously. The *William A. Jamison* was extensively damaged with a huge hole in her side and was a total loss. **Below:** The British steamship *Iperia* went ashore twelve miles north of Barnegat, New Jersey on June 15, 1919. Tugs from the Merritt & Chapman Wrecking Company hooked on to her and pulled her off the next day with little damage.

Above: The *SS Point Comfort* was wrecked on Esopus Island on the night of September 17, 1919 while heading up river. The crew lost their way in heavy fog and ran the steamer on the rocks near Hyde Park. There were no injuries. The crew put over a lifeboat and rowed ashore. The vessel never sailed again. She slowly disintegrated where she lay on the rocks at the northern end of Esopus Island. **Below:** The schooner barge *Lewis H. St. John,* sank off Ellis Island in New York harbor after being in collision with the steamer *Madison* during the night of Tuesday, December 9, 1919. She was raised and continued in service until April 24, 1924, when she stranded in Lubec Bay, Maine.

Above: The 3,269 ton coastal steamer *Princess Anne* went up on Rockaway Shoals in stormy weather on February 6, 1920. There were forty passengers and sixty-four crewmen aboard. **Below:** Because of the storm and flooding in the hold, all power was lost and communications were cut off. The snow and ice prevented any rescue until two days later when a Coast Guard crew reached the ship and took off the passengers and twenty crewmen.

A heavy snowstorm and northeast gale was raging along the coast on February 6, 1920 when the steamship *Princess Anne* of the Old Dominion line, lost her bearings and went aground on Rockaway Shoals, four and a half miles WSW of the Rockaway beach Coast Guard station. During the storm, the station crew made three attempts to launch their surfboat and go out to the grounded steamer but each time, they were thrown back on the beach by the high surf. On the following day, the Coast Guardsmen boarded a police motor launch and went to the steamer. Forty passengers and twenty crewmen were brought ashore on the police boat. The rest of the crew remained aboard to assist wreckers in refloating the vessel.

When the passengers landed in New York, they told of the hardships endured aboard the ship with no heat and little food. Some of the passengers suffered from various illnesses because of the accident. They had been on the ship for three days coming up from Norfolk, Virginia, in storm tossed waters. The trip usually takes twenty hours but the storm delayed the passage. Weather conditions made observations impossible necessitating the crew to navigate by dead reckoning.

The condition of the *Princess Anne* was tenuous. Her number 3 hold was full of water and the hull was pounding hard in the storm tossed waves on the shoals. The weather improved little and the Coast Guard cutter *Manhattan* tried to haul the ship off the sandbars. There were six other steamboats caught in the ice at the same time in Long Island Sound and steamship lines suspended service until the weather improved. On February 10th the New York Maritime Register reported: "The Old Dominion Line steamer *Princess Anne* is pounding to pieces today on the inner bar off Rockaway Point. Agents of the Merritt & Chapman Wrecking Company said that some of the cargo which was floating might be salvaged if favorable weather conditions prevailed." The ship later broke in half and was a total wreck.

A massive explosion occurred at Black Tom, New Jersey on January 29, 1916. The main terminal for shipment of arms to Europe for the war suffered a huge loss when a fire of undetermined origin touched off the blast. A few days later divers were recovering shells from the bottom and men above stacked them up on a barge.

Chapter Nine

War always adds misery to the lives that it touches. In addition to the maritime losses normally suffered along our eastern coastline, World War One brought an increase in shipping losses. During the war years, New York waters were troubled and saw their share of maritime depredations. Even before our entry into the war we felt its ramifications. Although the war started in 1914, the United States didn't declare war on Germany until 1917. Never-the-less, we felt the heat of war and became victimized before the latter date.

On January 3, 1915, an explosion of mysterious origin occurred on the *SS Orton* that was docked at Erie Basin. During the months that followed, bombs were found on board vessels carrying cargo to the Allies. Fires also began to break out on many ships with similar cargoes. Much of this sabotage was traced to a group of German sympathizers who used a German vessel as a workshop. It was estimated that their sabotage had been successful on 36 vessels with cargo losses running into the millions of dollars. The sinking of the huge liner *SS Lusitania* on May 7, 1915, off the coast of Ireland, cost 1,198 lives, 124 of which were American. This tragedy shocked many American citizens and cost the German government a great deal of sympathy here in the United States.

One of the worst disasters that occurred before we entered the war was the terrible explosion at Black Tom, New Jersey on January 29, 1916. Black Tom was a peninsula that extended for about a mile from Jersey City out into the entrance of the Hudson River. It was located directly in back of the Statue of Liberty. It was the main terminal in the United States for the shipment of arms and ammunition to the wartime Allies. The piers at Black Tom were owned by the Lehigh Valley Railroad Company. On the night of July 29, there were 34 railroad carloads of ammunition waiting at the wharves to be loaded on vessels bound for Europe. In addition to the freight cars, there were close to ten barges tied to the piers and most of these were loaded with high explosives.

At 12:45 a.m., watchmen on the wharves noticed a fire in one of the cars of ammunition. They immediately turned in an alarm and then ran for their lives. An hour and twenty three minutes later there was a tremendous blast that was quickly followed by an even heavier detonation. Both were felt as far as 20 miles away, shattering windows, shaking tall buildings and doing extensive property damage. Two million pounds of high explosives had blown up, leveling nearby buildings, blowing people out of their beds and sending flames and bursting shells high into the night sky. For a considerable period of time, artillery shells continued to explode like huge firecrackers. The sky turned red from the fires that followed. Surprisingly, and due probably to the late hour of the blast, only a few people were killed. However, the damage in property loss amounted to 22 million dollars. Although sabotage was suspected, it was never proven. Whoever or whatever started the fire in the box-car is still unknown.

Following our declaration of war with Germany, seven U-boats were sent across the Atlantic in 1918 to harass and sink our shipping. Several of these were quite successful in their efforts. With the waters off New York being a natural target, shipping interests in the area were indeed fearful for the safety of their vessels, cargoes and crews. The U-151, in command of Commander Von Nostitz, operated off our eastern coast from May 15 to July 1. A considerable amount of this time was spent lurking in the shipping lanes off Long Island and New Jersey. The U-151 sank over twenty ships and laid mines off New York harbor and Delaware Bay. These mines accounted for the loss of four more vessels.

Above: On the evening trip from New York to Bridgeport, Connecticut on February 4, 1920, the steamer *Maine* ran into thick pack ice in Long Island Sound. The ice was over four feet thick and stopped up the condenser water intake on the ship. The vessel lost power and was stopped in the ice. A northeast snowstorm was raging. The turn of the tide carried the *Maine* onto a ledge near Execution Rocks punching a hole in her bottom and filling the lower deck. The steamer settled to the bottom with the water above the freight deck. The passengers and crew were stranded on board for three days without much heat until a freight lighter worked her way to the steamer through the ice and removed the passengers, plus a dozen or so horses. Officials of the New England Steamship Company surveyed the steamer and found that salvage was going to be too expensive so they ordered her stripped and abandoned. **Below:** Because of the danger of fire and the proximity to the lighthouse, the upper wooden superstructure was burned to get rid of it. With the wind just right, wreckers touched off the wood and within eight minutes the whole vessel was involved. The fuel was eastern white pine, 29 years old with several coats of white paint. Within a few hours, all of the wood was burned away leaving metal parts for salvage. *Photos courtesy of Bob Beattie.*

A huge steel net was stretched across the mouth of New York harbor. Guns were installed in forts near the harbor entrance and in forts at the eastern entrance to Long Island Sound. There were also forts guarding the East River where it connected with the sound. Sixteen tugs that were based at Staten Island were commandeered as mine sweepers. Mines outside of Sandy Hook were exploded in daily sweeping operations. However, not all were found and destroyed. On July 19, 1918, the U.S. armored cruiser *San Diego* was sunk by a mine. She was only ten miles southeast of Fire Island. Of the 1,189 men on board, only six lost their lives and six others were wounded.

At the conclusion of World War One, peaceful operations came once more and our armed forces were reduced in number. However, there was one branch that was soon to renew its efforts. The United States Coast Guard was called upon to enter another battle in the 1920's that was to continue for almost fourteen years. The prohibition of the importation, sale or manufacture of intoxicating beverages went into effect in the United States on January 16, 1920. The U.S. Coast Guard was one of the chief agencies in the enforcement of the National Prohibition Act, customarily referred to as the Volstead Act.

As soon as anything is made illegal, there are bound to spring up those who will engage in black market operations and make a business out of supplying the illegal goods. So it proved with alcohol. The best liquors to be had were generally those supplied to us by foreign countries and in no time, the "Rum Runner" became a fact of life along our eastern coastlines. At first, the lot of the rum runner was an easy one. From the moment that "booze" had been banned, it seemed to increase in popularity. The demand grew rapidly and "stills" and "speak easy's" began to operate throughout the country. "Rot gut" was a term applied to some of the produce made in many home operated outfits. Aside from its bad taste, the drinking of "moonshine" could be dangerous to the health of the consumer. As most "bootleggers" would tell their customers: "The good stuff comes from abroad".

Vessels of all kinds which were capable of making an ocean passage were loaded with whiskey, rum and liquors of many types and varieties. From ports in Europe, St. Pierre et Miquelon and the Caribbean they came in great numbers. Steamers, large and small schooners, fishing boats and even tugs and barges were all used to haul illegal spirits into American waters. At first, the Coast Guard just didn't have the material or manpower to handle the flood of incoming "booze". The rum runners often brazenly ran their cargoes into a little used coastal location and unloaded into waiting trucks. Frequently, they were aided and abetted by sympathetic shore residents who resented the business of prohibition in its entirety.

As the Coast Guard warmed up to its task, the suppliers and those who landed the contraband on the beach found that their work was becoming more difficult. The larger supply vessels were forced to lay outside of Sandy Hook, just beyond the three mile limit where they comfortably bobbed about while waiting for the swift "buy boats" from shore to come alongside and relieve them of a portion of their cargo. This fleet of outside vessels became known as "rum row". The "buy boats" in most cases were swift speed boats whose powerful engines could outrun anything the Coast Guard would put in pursuit. Many of these small boats were armor plated in and around their control areas.

The whiskey being delivered was customarily packed in wooden crates with each bottle being protected by a straw wrapping. Nighttime was primarily best suited to the purposes of the rum runners whose vessels were termed "blacks" by the patrolling Coast Guard crews. After sneaking out to rum row after dark, the buy boats conducted their business with the supply boats on a strictly cash and carry basis. After the cash had changed hands the cases of liquor were hoisted out into the smaller boats and they sped off into the night to pre-arranged destinations on shore. The Coast Guard had about 30 patrol boats and cutters attached to the Port of New York during prohibition and they were constantly in use. Not only did they have the rum runners to watch out for but they also had the usual problems with storms, shipwreck and other "normal" difficulties that had to be attended to during the course of daily events. The New York District extended from Delaware to Rhode Island. This was a very wide area to be patrolled. It was a tough and often thankless job. The language that passed back and forth between Coast Guard crewmen and boats being inspected or checked can best be imagined rather than written.

After the passage of a few years, the supply boats were forced further out to sea. They had to, then, wait outside the 12 mile limit. There were those who thought that this might slow down the trade. Lengthening the trip out to sea, however, did not deter the ambitious. Bigger and faster

Above: The Munson Line steamer *Moccasin* sank at her pier in Brooklyn, on March 2, 1920. Reports of an organized plot to damage ships formerly under the German flag were being investigated by the United States Shipping Board. **Below:** Cause of the sinking was laid to an open sea cock but this was not confirmed.

speed boats were added to the fleet of buy boats and their armor plating was increased. In 1924, part of the U.S. Navy's fleet of inactive destroyers was turned over to the Coast Guard to add to their numbers in an effort to strengthen the war on rum runners. Twenty destroyers were in the first group and six more were added in 1926. These larger vessels then began a regular picketing of the vessels waiting out on rum row.

Serious problems began to mount for the rum runners. In addition to the increasing effectiveness of the Coast Guard, hijackers began to appear on the scene. Outright piracy would probably be a more correct term describing the actions of the newcomers. Often disguising themselves as buy boats, these pirates earned for themselves the picturesque name of 'Go Through Guys". They would usually wait until most of the cargo on the supply boat had been unloaded and there was an undoubtedly large amount of money on board. Then, pulling alongside their victim, they would go aboard ostensibly to make a regular buy. Once on board, guns were drawn and the supply ship was robbed of the cash. Often, it was also relieved of any remaining liquor. These robberies frequently erupted into pitched gun battles, leaving many on both sides either wounded or killed. If the supply ship won, the bodies of the pirates were simply thrown overboard to feed the sharks. If the pirates won, the crew members were tossed over the side and the vessel was abandoned. There were several cases where the larger supply boats were found abandoned and floating as derelicts with nothing but dozens of bullet holes left to tell the tale of robbery and murder. Although the rum runners had radios, they couldn't very well call the Coast Guard for help.

One of the most brazen attempts to land liquor in New York occurred on the night of July 3, 1927. The 793 ton British freighter *Economy* was spotted trying to sneak into the harbor under the cover of very low visibility. With only a couple of lights dimly showing she was spotted by a 36-foot patrol boat. The patrol boat immediately gave chase and ordered the steamer to stop. Their orders were ignored. Ensign Charles L. Duke then fired several shots from his revolver which were also ignored. The Coast Guardsmen then pulled their patrol boat alongside the recalcitrant steamer and Ensign Duke vaulted on board. With his revolver in hand he made his way toward the pilot house. A burly crewman tried to stop Duke and he hit him over the head with his pistol. Upon reaching the pilot house, Ensign Duke held additional members of the ship's crew at bay with only three shots remaining in his revolver. He ran the steamer aground off Robbins Reef, in ten feet of water. He then waited for sunrise and help to arrive. There were over 20 men taken into custody in this particular incident.

There were a great many colorful characters whose reputations were spawned during the days of prohibition. Certainly one of the most well known was Captain Bill McCoy. The term "the real McCoy", came from the fact that Captain McCoy sold only the best and dealt fairly with his customers. McCoy started out early in the rum running business with the schooner *Henry L. Marshall.* In 1921, he bought his beloved fishing schooner *Arethusa,* which was subsequently named *Tomoka.*

During the summer of 1921, the *Marshall* was sighted by the cutter *Seneca* and was captured about four miles off Atlantic City, New Jersey. In as much as the *Henry L. Marshall* had been placed under British registry, her capture raised an uncomfortable international incident. In 1923, the *Tomoka* was captured by the *Seneca* with part of a load of booze off Seabright, New Jersey. Captain McCoy was arrested after operating a third schooner and spent nine months in the penitentiary at Atlanta. Upon his release, he sold his vessel interests and retired to Florida.

For sure, running rum was a risky business but the profits were huge. When caught by a patrolling Coast Guard vessel, the crews on the rum runners frequently tried to get rid of the evidence by throwing their cargoes overboard. Sometimes this worked and at other times it didn't. If they were caught with the goods, they faced a prison sentence and the confiscation of their vessel. In spite of the consequences, there were many who were more than willing to try their luck.

On December 5, 1933, the 21st amendment to the U.S. Constitution went into effect repealing the 18th amendment and ending prohibition. The "Noble Experiment" as President Herbert Hoover called it, had ended in failure.

Above: The Norwegian steamship *Hallfried* was destroyed by fire on April 20, 1920 while lying beside pier 5 at the Bush Terminal in Brooklyn. **Below:** Several barges were seriously damaged in the fire which was out of control before tugs and fireboats contained it with water.

Above: New York fireboats contained the blaze aboard the *Hallfried* but the ship was a burned out hulk when the fire was finally extinguished. **Below:** Tugboats towed the ship out and beached her on a mud bank prior to being floated and placed alongside a pier to unload the remaining cargo

Above: The 2,329 ton freighter *Lake Deval* stranded on the beach near Southampton, Long Island on March 12, 1920. The vessel was underway very slowly, through heavy fog when the grounding occurred. The ship was sighted by a member of the Meadow House Club near Southampton who gave the alarm. A strong southeast wind caused the ship to develop a starboard list. Later the wind shifted and the list was corrected. There were 34 persons on board the freighter and all were rescued by the Coast Guard. The vessel lay on the shore for a week. She was refloated on March 20th. **Below:** Life Savers from the Bay Shore Life Saving Station pose for the photographer beside their lifeboat after a drill. The men wore the old style cork life-jackets and hip boots during drills. *Photo by Anderson, Courtesy of the Suffolk Marine Museum, West Sayville, Long Island, New York.*

Above: The divers line up for a photograph aboard the Merritt & Chapman Derrick & Wrecking Company barge MONARCH. Twenty-one men with their diving gear and helmets. It was a tough job carried out in all kinds of weather, occasionally bad. **Below:** An explosion aboard the steamship *El Mundo* occurred on November 10, 1920 while she was laying beside a pier in New York City. The vessel was towed out and beached on a shoal in the harbor. The damage was limited and the ship was refloated on the 19th by the Merritt & Chapman Wrecking Company. She was taken to a dry-dock.

Above: Built in Portsmouth, New Hampshire between 1819 and 1825, the *New Hampshire,* later the *Granite State,* a 74 gun ship of the line was being used by the New York state naval militia as a barracks ship when she caught fire on May 23, 1921, and sank at the pier on the Hudson River. She was raised and sold for scrap. The ship was being towed to the Bay of Fundy when she sank in a storm off Graves Island near Cape Ann, Massachusetts. New England's *Scuba* divers have brought up many copper spikes from this vessel, said to have been wrought in Paul Revere's foundry. **Below:** A diver descending a ladder beside a Merritt & Chapman Company barge to dive on the sunken tugboat *Julia C. Moran* on July 20. 1921.

Above: At 1:30 a.m., Sunday September 18, 1921, about six miles south of Montauk Shoals off Long Island in thick fog, the steam collier *Malden* was in collision with the *S.S. Johancy.* The *Malden* suffered a large hole in her port side forward of the bridge. An SOS was sent out and salvage tugs arrived on scene the next morning to take the *Malden* in tow. **Below:** That evening, the ship sank on a sand bar just east of Washington Shoal, near Montauk Point. After she lay on the bar a few days, it was decided to abandon the vessel. Later the Coast Guard destroyed her as a menace to navigation. *Photo by Bob Beattie.*

On December 9, 1921, the submarine S-48, while operating with a civilian crew, was undergoing trials in Long Island Sound, when a leak was discovered. A large amount of water seeped in. When it came in contact with the batteries, chlorine gas was formed and the vessel would not surface. The crew lightnened the bow compartment until it projected above water. The 40 men aboard crawled out through a torpedo tube and clung to the hull for eight hours until a passing tug picked them up. *Photo courtesy of the Naval Historical Museum, Washington, D.C.*

Above: The Merritt & Chapman Wrecking Company barges MONARCH and CENTURY put cables on the submarine S-48 and raised her on an almost even keel. The sub was taken to a shipyard for repairs. **Below:** Another one of the wrecking vessels of the Merritt & Chapman Wrecking Company showing the galloping horse flag, was the salvage vessel *Rescue*.

Above: The Great Lakes Dredge and Dock Company dredge CREST working to keep the channels deep enough for the maritime traffic in and around the New York waters. Below: The four masted schooner *Charles A. Dean* was almost lost in a collision on the night of March 24, 1922 off the New Jersey coast. The United Fruit steamer *Metapan* rammed into the sailing vessel just after midnight in heavy fog, eighty miles south of the Ambrose Channel lightship. An S O S radio call was sent to the Coast Guard cutter Gresham which was towing a disabled Spanish steamer into New York. The commander of the cutter replied that he would drop the steamer at the Scotland Lightship and then pick up the *Charles A. Dean*. Passengers aboard the Metapan were awakened by the collision and several men complained of nervousness and demanded that the bar be opened. They stormed the tavern and started to sing "How Dry I Am". This annoyed the other passengers trying to go back to sleep. The United Fruit steamer *Metapan* is the same one appearing on earlier pages of this book, sunk twice, once by collision.

The four masted Canadian schooner *Bessie A. White* went aground in heavy fog a mile west of Smith's Point, Long Island on February 6, 1922. The crew launched two boats and came to shore. One boat capsized in the surf with minor injuries to one man. The vessel had fifteen hundred tons of coal aboard. Wreckers tried to save the ship but she was subsequently a total loss. *Photo courtesy of the Mariners Museum, Newport News, Virginia.*

Two Long Island Sound vessels grounded on the Sunken Meadows of Hell Gate on April 6, 1922 in dense fog. The Colonial Line steamboat *Concord,* above with 100 passengers and the N.E. Steamship Line freight boat *City of Brockton,* below, were aground within twenty-five feet of each other. The Fall River liner *Providence* anchored before she ran aground after hearing the distress signals of the other two. When the fog lifted the three vessels were in close proximity in the narrow passage. The passengers on the *Concord,* mostly women and children were removed safely. The two grounded ships were floated at six in the evening at high tide.

Above: About 3 a.m. on May 19, 1922, the U.S. Navy *Eagle Boat #17* ran aground near Ammagansett, Long Island. The Navy craft was in pursuit of a rumrunner near the shore in thick weather. The rummy lured the ship too close to shore and she sheared off her propeller trying to back out off the bar. **Below:** The 64-man crew was rescued by the Coast Guard from the Georgica Station with the breeches buoy. The ship was a total loss. The rumrunner had an easy escape. *Photo by Bob Beattie.*

Above: The four masted schooner *Orlando V. Wooten,* out of Jacksonville, Florida, with a load of lumber for New York City went aground in thick fog at Barnegat, New Jersey on April 7, 1922. A Coast Guard crew from the Forked River station went to the schooner but the crew refused to leave. A tug and lighter from New York arrived to take the cargo off and two cutters, The *Kickapoo* and *Gresham* failed to move the vessel from the tenacious sands of the New Jersey shore. Some of the cargo of lumber was saved but the schooner was a total loss. **Below:** The Boston Steamer *Mohawk* stranded on the rocks in the Kill Van Kull on August 9, 1922. A salvage vessel from the Merritt & Chapman Wrecking Company went alongside the *Mohawk* but could not haul her off. The 535 ton vessel broke in half and was abandoned by her owners. She was stripped and left to rot away along the shore.

Above: The two masted barge *Albany* and the three masted *Number Seventeen* were sunk on Man-O-War reef in the East River on November 16, 1922. **Below:** Both vessels were a total loss. The East River can be a challenging passage for any tug boat captain towing barges, especially at Hell Gate.

The steamer *Sagua* was at a shipyard in New Jersey when she caught fire and burned. A report in the New York Maritime Register on February 21, 1923 outlined the damage as a result of the flames "Stmr Sagua, while being converted to an oil burner at the Fletcher's works, Hoboken, NJ, took fire February 16 and was badly damaged throughout. The stmr careened and was almost on her beam ends by the time the fire was extinguished; the fire was principally in Nos 1 and 2 holds."

Above: The British steamship *Mayari,* bound from Boston for New York, grounded on the west side of Harts Island on February 21, 1923 and was high on the rocky shore. A period of low tides prevented salvagers from refloating the vessel until February 27th when she was pulled off. **Below:** The Italian freighter *Buckleigh* went aground near Long Beach, Long Island on March 16, 1923 in dense fog. The vessel was boarded by Coast Guards men but the Captain declined any aid until he received instructions from his agent and he refused to allow his crewmen to be landed. The vessel was refloated by the Merritt Chapman & Scott Wrecking Company on March 30th and towed to New York City.

The Nova Scotia built four-masted schooner *Ada Tower* came ashore at Sayville, Long Island on May 23, 1923. The Bay of Fundy vessels were built to take good ground without damaging their hulls. The sandy shores of Long Island did no damage to the vessel and on May 29th, the *Tower* was pulled off by the Merritt Chapman & Scott Wrecking Company and towed to Clifton, Staten Island.

The steamer *Squantum* was wrecked at 9th street, Brooklyn on January 16, 1924. The vessel was smashed against the shore in a bad northeast storm and was a total loss.

The American liner *Leviathan* went aground near Robbins Reef Light on December 21, 1923 but was floated off a few hours later by tugboats. What seemed at the time to be a minor occurrence turned out to be major destruction on the Passiac Valley sewer which runs under the harbor. Somewhat later, the Merritt Chapman & Scott wrecking company brought up a damaged section of the sewer line. The break in the line allowed raw untreated sewerage into New York harbor. Damage to the pipe by the ship was estimated to be in excess of $100,000.

Above: The coastal tanker *Anahuac* on a voyage from Philadelphia to Providence went ashore near Bellport, Long Island on April 6, 1924 and lay broadside to the beach. The Merritt Chapman & Scott wrecking steamer *Resolute* went to the scene to aid in salvage. The vessel was refloated on the morning of April 18th and towed to Staten Island. *Photo courtesy of the Mystic Seaport Museum, Mystic, Connecticut.* **Below:** The *SS Grand Republic,* sister ship to the *General Slocum* sunk on the left in the photo above, was one of the five vessels destroyed by fire early in the morning of April 26, 1924 at their winter berth in the Hudson River off 157th Street. The fire started in the *SS C.A.M. Church* and spread to the *SS Highlander* and the lighter Nassau and the towboat *Barton.* Several thousand persons were attracted to the scene by the flames leaping into the air. Fire companies from all over the city responded to additional alarms but the boats could not be saved. *Photo courtesy of the Steamship Historical Society.*

The steamer *Bermudez* sank at the Erie Basin in Brooklyn on March 16, 1924. The stern of the vessel rested on the bottom while the bow was still afloat. The Merritt & Chapman Wrecking Company put pumps aboard the ship and refloated her.

Above: The passenger steamer *Pastime* struck a rock at Norton's Point on July 8, 1925 and stove a hole in her hull. There were 67 passengers and 22 crewmen aboard when the accident occurred. The vessel was run inshore where she was berthed at a coal company pier, while the passengers landed safely. The *Pastime* was pumped out by the salvage vessel *Citizen* and taken to a dry dock for repairs. **Below:** The British freighter *City of Norwich,* in ballast and carrying a crew of 65 lost her way in fog and ran aground early on the morning of December 1, 1926 at Sayville, on Long Island. Coast Guard crewmen from the Blue Point station fired a line out to the grounded vessel and rigged the breeches buoy. The steamer was lying easy and no one came ashore. Later a cutter from Staten Island pulled the ship off without damage.

Above: The freighter *Hilton* of the Bull Line struck an obstruction in the Kill Van Kull Channel off the mouth of Woodbridge Creek on February 27, 1927. The ship was run on the mud flats near the mouth of the creek where she sank by the stern. There was extensive damage to the cargo of phosphate rock. The steamer was on a voyage from Tampa, Florida to Carteret, New Jersey. The vessel was unloaded and later converted to a barge. *Photo courtesy of Mariners Museum, Newport News, Virginia.* **Below:** The steam tug *Two Brothers* ran up on a sandbar off Rockaway Point on April 20, 1928 and was a total loss. The tugs engines had failed. She broke loose while being towed by another tug and drifted on the bar. The heavy seas pounded the vessel to pieces. Five men on board were rescued by the Coast Guard surfboat from the Rockaway Point station. *Photo courtesy of the U.S. Coast Guard, Washington, D.C.*

Above: Late on the night of March 18, 1931, the British freighter *Silveryew* rammed head-on into the small coastal freighter *Arminda* in lower New York harbor. Officials could not determine the cause of the accident as it was a clear night and visibility was good. Seven men asleep in the foc'sle were injured, one seriously, with a broken back, when the collision occurred. The extent of the damage is clearly visible with the ship in dry-dock. *Photo courtesy of the Steamship Historical Society of America, Viez collection.* **Below:** Two side-wheel steamboats were lost to fire on the morning of May 9, 1932 when the *Albertina* caught fire and the flames spread to the *Sea Bird,* while both vessels were moored to lumber piers at 152nd Street on the East River in New York. Fire fighters poured water on the smoldering hull of the *Sea Bird* while all that can be seen of the *Albertina* is the walking beam in the smoky background. *Photo courtesy of the Peabody Museum of Salem, Salem, Massachusetts.*

Above: The fishing vessel *Anna and Ella* went ashore on Loveladies Island near the Coast Guard station, two and a half miles south of Barnegat Inlet in New Jersey on March 7, 1933. The vessel was pulled off the beach and continued fishing until January 23, 1936 when she collided with the steamship *Edward Luckenbach* and was lost with her crew of six men. **Below:** The stern of the United Fruit steamship *Atenas* settled to the bottom beside the North River pier in New York following a six hour battle by land and marine fire forces to put out the fire in the after holds. The blaze of undetermined origin occurred on July 27, 1934, and caused a half million dollar loss. The ship was later raised and repaired. *Photo courtesy of the Mariners Museum, Newport News, Virginia.*

Passengers crossing the Atlantic in the 1930's still preferred the comfort of the big ocean liners. By then, navigations aids along with radio communication had greatly improved. On May 15, 1934, the White Star liner *Olympic* rammed and sank the Nantucket Lightship. The liner was following the radio beacon from the lighthsip during a thick fog. The huge liner cut the tiny vessel in two. Seven men died and four were rescued. *Drawing by Paul C. Morris.*

Above: The Ward Line steamer *Morro Castle* was a luxurious liner, very popular for tropical cruises even in the depression times of the 1930's. *Photo courtesy of the Steamship Historical Society of America.* **Below:** There was, however, what sailors called a "jinx" connected with the ship. Several accidents and minor fires plagued the vessel throughout her career. *Photo courtesy of the Mariners Museum, Newport News, Virginia.*

Chapter Ten

Fire at sea has always been an event greatly feared by anyone on or associated with ships. In the days of wooden ships and iron men there were a great many vessels and lives lost due to fires. Carelessness was usually the cause of most fires at sea but occasionally faulty construction or weather conditions were contributing factors. Sometimes a combination of both would lead to a fire. Spontaneous combustion on vessels long at sea with cargoes such as coal was also not uncommon.

If a burning vessel was supplied with adequate lifeboats and life preservers, passengers and crew had a chance to survive. If the burning vessel happened to be far at sea and in an area that was outside of any of the normally used shipping lanes, survival in a lifeboat could be difficult; floating in a life preserver was often only a prelude to a lingering death.

Fires on board ships that were anchored or tied up to a wharf were often serious enough to cause the loss of the vessel. But if warned in time, generally most of the people on board would make good their escape. Circumstances played a great part in the possible survival from a fire for those on board ship.

Weather conditions, the motion of the vessel, whether it was under way or lying still, made a difference as to the successful evacuation of the ship. People jumping off a moving vessel whose engines and propellers or paddle wheels were turning were frequently pulled into the vortex and killed. Lifeboats lowered while the ship was under way were often slammed into the side or swung broadside and pulled over and swamped.

Cool heads on the part of ship's officers often meant the saving of many lives. Fire on shipboard occasionally led to panic on the part of passengers and crew. Panic and loss of reason frequently led to loss of life. Outright cowardice on the part of crew members in several cases cost the lives of terrified passengers. The motto of the sea was "women and children first". Those crewmen who added, "after me", were treated with contempt in subsequent disaster investigations. Those who showed blatant disregard for passengers during marine disasters were later disgraced publicly and some were sentenced to prison terms.

New York harbor and its approaches had many marine conflagrations over the period of it's long history. Ships tied to docks and the docks themselves, frequently went up in smoke when a fire got out of control. Also there were ships that were leaving or heading toward the port which for one reason or another caught fire with resulting loss of life.

One terrible marine fire that I remember very well from my days as a youngster was the luxury liner *Morro Castle* which burned off Asbury Park, New Jersey, on September 8, 1934. It was an event that made headlines in all the newspapers for many weeks. It attracted many visitors to the coast of New Jersey to view the smoldering hulk as it lay just off the beach at the park. My family was there at Asbury Park and the sight of the charred and still burning liner with its twisted metal lifeboats dangling over the side was something not likely to be forgotten.

The *Morro Castle* was a fairly new liner when she burned. She had been built in 1930 for the American Ward Line at a cost of $4,800,000, and at the time of her launching was considered one of the finest coastal liners afloat. She was 508 feet in overall length, measured 11,520 gross tons and had three decks fitted out to carry 490 passengers.

As the *Titanic* was considered unsinkable, the *Morro Castle* was thought to be safe from fire. She was equipped with smoke detectors, fire doors, fire hoses and extinguishers. An automatic fire alarm was built into each stateroom, the officers quarters and the radio room. There were also fire resisting partitions and doors built in at 130 foot intervals. In addition to all of her fire fighting equipment, the liner also carried more than enough lifeboats and life jackets for all the passengers and crew. Yet with all of these safety devices, the *Morro Castle* was seriously flawed.

Early in the morning of September 8, 1934, the *Morro Castle* caught fire. The crew failed to fight the fire correctly and soon the entire vessel was involved. The Coast Guard Cutter *Tampa* attempted to tow the *Morro Castle* to New York harbor but the cable broke. The burned out hulk drifted ashore in front of the Convention Hall at Asbury Park, New Jersey. *Photo courtesy of the Mariners Museum, Newport News, Virginia.*

Her interior compartments were partitioned with wood. Plywood had been used extensively in the construction of staterooms, lounges and other public rooms. None of the public rooms were equipped with fire alarms. In addition, all of the stairways between decks were open and lined with combustible material. Along with being lavishly fitted out, the big liner was also fast. She ran regularly from New York to Havana Cuba. On her maiden trip in 1930, she made the passage in 58 hours and 40 minutes, with an average speed of 20.5 knots. She was also fitted out for fun. The population of the United States in the early 1930's was still reeling from the great depression. Those who went aboard the *Morro Castle* for a week's romp, wanted to forget their troubles and have a good time. The crew on the big ship was expected to cater to those passengers who were looking for "happier days".

On her return trip from Havana in September of 1934, there was an underlying feeling of discontent smoldering among some of the crew members. A strike had been threatened before the ship had left from New York and Captain Robert Wilmott was worried. His worries were further heightened when a mysterious fire broke out the second day from Havana. It was quickly extinguished. On September 7, Captain Wilmott suddenly and mysteriously died. The liner was off the coast of New Jersey that evening and Chief Officer William Warms then took over command of the ship. The death of the captain put a damper on part of the last night out proceedings. However, some of the passengers and crew did get together in the lounge for a little socializing and drinking.

At 2:45 a.m., while the ship was heading into a choppy sea from a northeast wind, a passenger informed assistant steward Donald Campbell that there was a fire in the ship's writing room. He immediately checked and found that the writing room on B deck, port side, was indeed blazing. He turned in an alarm and then tried to fight the fire with a portable fire extinguisher. His efforts were futile.

There were 318 passengers on board the ship returning from a eight-day holiday cruise to Havana Cuba. One hundred and thirty-four persons were lost that night in the fire. A total of 413 were rescued. The day after the ship came ashore at Asbury Park, thousands of spectators came to view the wreck. Most of the paint on the side of the ship had been burned off by the fire which is still smoldering in the photograph above. *Photo courtesy of the Mariners Museum, Newport News, Virginia.*

Hundreds of people climbed over the breakwater to get a closer look at the burning vessel so near to the beach. Among these were the Author, Paul C. Morris, in the photograph above with his brother Bill and Mother, Martha Morris in the far right side of the picture. *Photo by the late Paul C. Morris Sr.*

In ten minutes time the fire had gained considerably and a general alarm was sounded. Acting Captain Warms took over control in fighting the fire. Unfortunately, most of the efforts against the fire were on a rather haphazard basis and it was soon raging out of control. Passengers were hurriedly awakened and advised of the situation.

About twenty minutes after the first alarm, a radio call for assistance was sent out from the *Morro Castle.* By this time, she was blazing fiercely and the light from the fire could be seen from shore. She was still headed in a northeasterly direction with no slack in her speed and the driving wind through broken windows further fanned the flames. The liner was eventually turned and headed in toward the Jersey shore. She didn't get far. Around 3:31 a.m., the ship lost power and the anchor was dropped which again brought her bow into the wind. About this time, confusion reigned supreme on the burning vessel.

Although some passengers were trapped below decks, others managed to reach the boat decks and a few lifeboats were launched. Number 1 lifeboat was lowered with 32 people, among whom were the Chief Engineer and one passenger. Few of the boats that did manage to get away were filled to capacity. While some crew members did try to help passengers, others thought only of themselves. Terror and pandemonium quickly followed.

With the fire roaring in the middle of the ship, the passengers located in back of it were steadily driven toward the stern. They soon found they had no other place to go. It was either jump overboard or burn. Jumping overboard from a thirty or forty foot height into choppy seas in the blackness of night took more than a little courage but there were many who did it. They were approximately seven miles from shore when the anchor was dropped and even the best swimmer would find such a distance exhausting under ordinary circumstances. Some were able to hang on to lines trailing over the stern and await rescue. Others wearing life jackets struck out from the ship which was dropping flaming hot embers on them in the water below. Some were rescued but many died.

A few days after the fires cooled down, people were still coming to see the remains of the ship. Spectators set up deck chairs to watch other spectators walking on the beach. A small sign on the beach (on the right) advertised a boat ride for fifty cents. The small dock in the center of the photograph was used as access for people to board the sightseeing boat which is shown coming around the stern of the ship. *Photo courtesy of the Mariners Museum, Newport News, Virginia.*

The ship stayed in the headlines for weeks, attracting more visitors to the beach at Asbury Park. City officials charged a 25 cent admission fee for Convention Hall Pier. They collected $2,800 and donated the money to needy relatives of those lost on the Morro Castle. *Photo courtesy of the Steamship Historical Society of America.*

Rescue ships that were in the area were quick to respond to the distress signals from the *Morro Castle*. The *Andrea F. Luckenbach, City of Savannah* and especially the *Monarch of Bermuda* were all helpful in saving lives. Shortly after noon on Saturday, the Coast Guard cutter *Tampa* attempted to tow the still blazing hulk into New York but the tow line broke fouling the cutter's propeller. The smoking derelict was then allowed to drift onto the beach at Asbury Park. For a while it was feared that she was going to crash into one of the large buildings located on the ocean side of the boardwalk but she "fetched up" in the sand about 60 or 70 feet away. There she lay for all to see.

The *Morro Castle* carried 316 passengers and 232 crew members on that last tragic voyage from Cuba. One hundred and twenty-four people died as a result of the fire or drowning. Eighty-nine were passengers and thirty-five were crewmen. There were weeks of inquiry afterwards and the acting captain and chief engineer were both tried in court and given prison sentences. Their sentences were later overturned by a superior court. The chief radio operator was made out to be a hero by the press and was even awarded some medals for his brave conduct. He was later sent to prison for an unrelated offense. Over a period of time, there were those who laid at his feet the blame for setting the fire. No one will ever know for sure. The chief radio operator died in prison in 1958 while serving time for a second offense.

While the burning of the *Morro Castle* was indeed one of the more spectacular tragedies that occurred off the port of New York, it did result in some good things happening. The maritime regulations governing the materials allowed on passenger carrying vessels was stiffened to prohibit any meaningful construction with combustible materials on large power vessels. Fire fighting systems had to be installed and crews trained in the use of these systems. Staircases had to be totally enclosed with fire doors that would be self closing. Escape routes had to be plainly marked. These and other regulations are on the plus side when evaluating the loss of the *Morro Castle*. Obviously, all the regulations in the world won't stop some accidents from happening. The big *Monarch of Bermuda*, which so valiantly saved so many of the *Morro Castle* survivors, was herself consumed by fire in 1947. Major shipwrecks occur almost every year. Collisions, strandings, sinkings and fires still happen to ships sailing the world's oceans.

Above: The crowd on the beach got a good close-up view of the ship and the damage it suffered from the fire. Some of the lifeboats were still in the davits. **Below:** The heat of the fire prevented crewmen from launching all of the boats and burned all of the paint off the side of the ship. *Photos courtesy of the Steamship Historical Society of America.*

A view of the bow hard up on the breakwater off shore from Asbury Park. The ship lay on the beach until it was hauled off by a salvage company. For the visitors to the beach it was an extraordinary experience to be so close to an authentic shipwreck of this magnitude. *Photo courtesy of the Steamship Historical Society of America.*

ACKNOWLEDGEMENTS

The collection of photographs in this book was completed over a period of several years. They came from several sources but the bulk of the material comes from the dispersed collection of the Merritt, Chapman & Scott Wrecking Company. There are many persons who helped in the acquisition of the pictures and we extend our appreciation to John Lochhead, former Librarian of the Mariners Museum in Newport News, Virginia; Norman J. Brouwer, Curator of Ships, South Street Museum, New York City; John Fish, Historical Maritime Group of New England; Robert Beattie of Belfast, Maine; Robert Scheina, Historian, U.S. Coast Guard; Bill Peterson, Photography Department, Mystic Seaport Museum; Laura Brown, Librarian for the Steamship Historical Society of America in Baltimore; Captain W.J.L. Parker, U.S.C.G. (Ret.); Gordon Caldwell and Bill Ewen. Valuable assistance was given by the staff of the G.W. Blount Library at Mystic Seaport Museum. Many kind thanks to all.

P.C.M. & W.P.Q.

An early view of the New York skyline, probably taken from a ferry boat approaching the tip of Manhattan. It was a busy place and the city continued its growth toward the sky. Three ferry boats are visible and the one on the left has automobiles of the late 1920's vintage.

BIBLIOGRAPHY

A Maritime History of New York, by the writers of the WPA
American Sailing Coasters of the North Atlantic, by Paul C. Morris
Flagships of the Line, by Milton H. Watson
Floating Palaces, by Roger Williams McAdams
Four Masted Schooners of the East Coast, by Paul C. Morris
From Sandy Hook to 62 Degrees, by Charles Edward Russell
Hudson River Day Line, by Donald C. Ringwald
Inventory of the Scott Company Papers by Charles R. Shultz
Life Saving Annual Reports, by the U.S. Government
Maritime New York, by Johnson and Lightfoot
Merchant Vessel of the United States, Annual reports by the U.S. Government
Ocean Liners, by Robert Wall
Perils of the Port of New York by Jeanette Edwards Rattray
Record of American and Foreign Shipping,
          Annual reports by the American Bureau of Shipping.
Salts of the Sound, by Rober Williams McAdams
Schooners and Schooner Barges, by Paul C. Morris
Ship Ashore, by Jeanette Edwards Rattray
Shipwrecks Around New England, by William P. Quinn
Shipwrecks Along the Atlantic Coast by William P. Quinn
Steamboat Days, by Fred Irving Dayton
The Boats We Rode, by Roberts and Gillespie
Tugboats, by Moran and Reid

Newspapers:

The New York Maritime Register
The New York Times

Libraries:

The Boston Public Library
The Falmouth Public Library
The New Bedford Public Library
The G.W. Blount Library at Mystic Seaport

Museums and Historical Societies:

Mystic Seaport Museum, Mystic Connecticut
South Street Seaport Museum, New York City
Steamship Historical Society, Baltimore, Maryland

APPENDIX

CHRONOLOGICAL LIST OF TOTAL WRECKS
IN NEW YORK WATERS

The following is a list of total wrecks in New York waters dating from the 1880's to the 1930's. The list is by no means complete as it is impossible to determine the exact number, or locations, of all the ships lost in the area between Montauk Point and Barnegat Inlet. The listing of more than six hundred wrecks represents about sixty percent of the total vessels lost during the time period indicated. The name of the ship and its rig, the date of the incident and the tonnage is cataloged in chronological order along with the approximate location of the wreck. The list is drawn from the annual reports of the U.S. Life Saving Service and the U.S. List of Merchant Vessels. For additional information, the casualty reports in the weekly editions of the New York Maritime Register show cause and results of most of the wrecks listed. Further research is recommended in the various Maritime Museums listed in the bibliography.

NAME	DATE	TONS	LOCATION
Sch Frank Pearsons	01 21 1880	83	Island Beach, N.J.
Sch Kate Newman	02 02 1880	146	2 Mi off New Jersey
Brig Augustina	02 03 1880	168	Monmouth Beach, N.J.
Sch. Stephen Harding	02 03 1880	305	Spermaceti Cove, N.J.
Sch Emma C. Babcock	02 03 1880	228	Monmouth Beach, N.J.
Sch George Taulane	02 03 1880	235	Green Isl. L.S.Sta, N.J.
Sch. Light Boat	02 03 1880	114	Long Branch, N.J.
Br. Brg Guisborough	02 03 1880	240	Sank in L.I. Sound.
Sch Ralph Howes	04 05 1880	143	Swan Point L.S.Sta, N.J.
Stmr Narragansett	04 29 1880	97	Georgica L.S.Sta, N.Y.
Bark Melchior	04 30 1880	986	Seabright LS Sta., N.J.
Stmr Narragansett	06 11 1880		Long Island Sound
Sch. Mary E. Turner	01 02 1881	112	Rockaway Beach, N.Y.
Bk. Josie T. Marshall	01 07 1881	1,072	Oak Island, N.Y.
Sch Loretta D. Fish	01 07 1881	316	Bridgehampton, N.Y.
Barge Veloz	02 12 1881	145	Point Pleasant, N.J.
Sch. Walter B. Chester	02 28 1881	429	Tiana L.S.Sta., N.Y.
Bark Ajace	03 04 1881	566	off Coney Island, N.Y.
Sch. P.M. Wheaton	10 26 1881	242	Collided, L.I. Sound, NY
Bg. Arctic	11 23 1881	274	Swan Point L.S.Sta., N.J.
Sch. J.H.M.	01 11 1882	194	Jones Inlet, East, N.Y.
Brig Mariposa	01 19 1882	298	Off Jones Inlet-East, NY
Ship Margaretha	01 27 1882	1,534	Smith's Point, N.Y.
Bark W.J. Stairs	03 02 1882	1,062	Long Branch, N.J.
Brig Thetis	03 16 1882	323	Ship Bottom, N.J.
Stmr Pliny	05 13 1882	1,060	Deal, N.J.
Sch Young Teaser	07 18 1882	156	Str. Smith's Point, N.Y.
Sch Copia	09 08 1882	135	Rockaway Beach, N.Y.
Brig Water Lily	12 09 1882	219	Forge River, L.I., N.Y.
Sch. Mabel Thomas	01 10 1883	336	Shark River LS Sta. N.J.

NAME	DATE	TONS	LOCATION
Stmr Granite State	05 18 1883	1,197	Burned in Conn. River.
Sch. Fannie A. Bailey	06 04 1883	258	Herford Inlet, N.J.
Sch. Laura Bridgman	06 19 1883	330	Shark River, N.J.
Stmr Riverdale	08 28 1883	433	New York harbor.
Sch. James Jones	10 31 1883	253	Barnaget Shoals
Dunderberg, No. 2	11 12 1883	601	L.I. Sound, sunk.
Barge Osprey	11 12 1883	468	L.I. Sound, sunk.
Barge Ida	11 12 1883	410	L.I. Sound, stranded.
Sch. Mary M. Hamilton	12 13 1883	110	L.I. Sound, sunk.
Bg. Albertine Meyer	02 06 1884	266	Barnegat Shoals, N.J.
Sch. Altavela	05 02 1884	183	Barnegat, N.J.
Sch. L. and A. Babcock	06 26 1884	255	Forked River L.S.S., N.J.
Sch. Deborah H. Diverty	07 01 1884	187	off Sea Isle, N.J.
Sch. Curtis Tilton	10 20 1884	243	Jones Inlet Bar.
Sch Alexander Harding	11 14 1884	325	Far Rockaway L.S.S.,N.Y.
Barge Saginaw	11 16 1884	269	E. River, New York
Stmr Guadaloupe	11 19 1884	2,839	Barnegat Shoals, N.J.
Bark Charlie Hickman	12 22 1884	903	Moriches, L.I., N.Y.
Sch Mary G. Farr	01 08 1885	330	Burned off N.J. shore
Sch. S.M. Thomas	02 10 1885	761	Point of Woods LS Sta, NY
Sch. Lida Babcock	02 15 1885	247	Forked River Sta, N.J.
Sch. Peacedale	11 23 1885	129	Ocean Grove, N.J.
Barge Cornelius Grinnell	11 23 1885	1,001	Off Highland Lite, N.J.
Ship Malta	11 24 1885	1,611	Ocean Beach, N.J.
Stmr West Jersey	12 25 1885	380	Tom's River LS Sta, N.J.
Bktn Charles Platt	02 10 1886	633	Ship Bottom L.S.Sta, N.J.
Bk. Kraljevica	02 11 1886	719	Barnegat Shoals
Br. Stmr Oregon	03 14 1886	7,500	Off Long Island, N.Y.
Ship Tsernogora	03 28 1886	1,252	Spring Lake L.S.Sta, N.J.
Sch. Pereaux	03 31 1886	146	Quogue L.S.Sta. N.Y.
Sch. Mary Haley	05 08 1886	205	Tom's River L.S.Sta, N.J.
Bktn James T. Abbott	06 24 1886	205	Georgica L.S.Sta, N.Y.
Sch. William A. Van Brunt	10 26 1886	260	Ship Bottom, N.J.
Bktn Lotus	01 03 1887	463	Long Beach L.S.Sta, N.Y.
Sch. Eva C. Yates	09 26 1887	360	Fire Island Bar, N.Y.
Sch. Nellie S. Jerrell	12 08 1887	349	Barnegat, N.J.
Sch Lena M. Cottingham	12 17 1887	210	5 Mi.-So.,Barnegat, N.J.
Barge Charles W. White	03 12 1888	236	Huntington, L.I. Sound
Sch. Emily and Jennie	04 08 1888	345	5 Mi So, Barnegat, N.J.
Ital. Bark Carrara	06 28 1888	434	Squan Shoals, N.J.
Sch. Andrew H. Edwards	06 28 1888	234	Seaside Park, N.J.
Stmr Bay Ridge,by fire.	08 11 1888	670	Glenwood, LI Sound, NY
Fr. Stmr Iberia	11 11 1888	1,388	Off Long Island, N.Y.
Stmr. George Appold	01 09 1889	1,456	Ditch Plain, N.Y.
Bark Violet	01 31 1889	846	Ship Bottom, N.J.
Ger. Ship J.W. Wendt	03 21 1889	2,369	Forked River, N.J.
Ger. Bark Erna	09 13 1889	582	Barnegat, N.J.
Stmr. Vertumnus	09 16 1889	742	Point Lookout, N.Y.
Sch. Sabao	10 12 1889	141	Jones Inlet Bar, N.Y.
Sch. Eva Diverty	10 15 1889	173	Eaton's Neck, N.Y.
Sch. Geo. P. Hallock	10 28 1889	333	off Tom's River, N.J.
Ger. Bk. Germania	11 27 1889	817	Long Branch, N.J.
Barge Amazon	01 24 1890	229	Race Rock Lite, LI Sound.
Sch. James B. Johnson	01 25 1890	148	Forked River, N.J.
Sch Lawrence N. McKenzie	03 21 1890	154	Forked River, N.J.
Scow E.T. Co. No. 28	06 04 1890	109	Hudson River, N.Y.
Stmr. Advance	09 02 1890	509	New York Bay, N.Y.
Brig Eugenie	10 28 1890	145	Jones Inlet Bar
Span. Stmr Viscaya	10 30 1890	2,458	12 Mi E. Barnegat, N.J.
Sch. Yale	12 26 1890	717	Deal Beach, N.J.

NAME	DATE	TONS	LOCATION
Can. Sch. Otter	01 13 1891	198	Bellport, L.I.
Str. City of Richmond	03 05 1891	1,001	Burned, N.Y. harbor.
Bk Umberto I Castellamare	03 13 1891	510	Romer Shoals, N.Y.
Brig Joseph Banigan	03 24 1891	177	Long Branch L.S.S., N.J.
Sch. Etna	10 07 1891	313	Sandy Hook, N.J.
Sch. Moses B. Bramhall	10 20 1891	345	Sandy Hook, N.J.
Sch. Adele Trudell	11 24 1891	157	Sandy Hook, N.J.
Bgntn Harry and Aubrey	01 25 1892	228	Blue Point L.S.S.,N.Y.
Sch. Mary E. Simmons	03 19 1892	200	Squan Beach, N.J.
Sch. Maggie P. Smith	05 20 1892	191	Mantoloking, N.J.
Sch. Jed Frye	06 13 1892	147	Long Island Sound, N.Y.
Bark Alice	02 06 1893	977	Ship Bottom, N.J.
Sch. Glenola	02 06 1893	124	Short Beach, L.I., N.Y.
Bgtn Ellie Carter	02 09 1893	147	Ship Bottom, N.J.
Sch. Elsie Fay	02 17 1893	172	Ditch Plain, L.I., N.Y.
Stmr Wells City	03 11 1893	1,136	Monmouth Beach, N.J.
Stmr. Gluckauf	03 29 1893	2,306	Bellport, L.I., N.Y.
Sch Magnolia	04 20 1893	277	Barnegat, N.J.
Sch Henry R. Congdon	04 20 1893	374	Deal, N.J.
Sch Hattie S. Williams	04 20 1893	898	Squan Beach, N.J.
Sch. Dixie	04 20 1893	298	Barnegat, N.J.
Barge Plymouth	04 20 1893	619	Barnegat, N.J.
Barge Lizzie Moses	04 20 1893	1,085	Long Branch, N.J.
Sch Thomas W. Haven	06 26 1893	314	Monmouth Beach, N.J.
Sch Lizzie Raymond	07 23 1893	119	Long Island Sound, N.Y.
Sch Lykens Valley	08 24 1893	841	Southampton, LI, N.Y.
Stmr Panther	08 24 1893	712	Southampton, LI, N.Y.
Relief Lightship # 37	08 24 1893	242	Five Fathom Bank, N.J.
Sch C. Henry Kirk	08 29 1893	184	Long Beach, L.I., N.Y.
Bark Martha P. Tucker	08 29 1893	635	Long Beach, LI, N.Y.
Sch. Richard B. Chute	11 16 1893	306	Short Beach, LI, N.Y.
Sch Louise H. Randall	11 28 1893	1,502	Moriches, LI, N.Y.
Sch Fannie J. Bartlett	01 16 1894	831	Hither Plain, LI, N.Y.
Sch Benjamin B. Church	04 07 1894	513	Mecox, LI, N.Y.
Sch Susan H. Ritchie	04 11 1894	541	Mantoloking, N.J.
Sch Albert W. Smith	04 11 1894	602	Squan Beach, N.J.
Sch Kate Markee	04 12 1894	504	Spermacetie Cove, N.J.
Sch A.F. Crocket	05 21 1894	434	Harvey Ceders, N.J.
Bark Emma T. Crowell	07 17 1894	1,136	12 Mi. So. Fire Isl. N.Y.
Sch. Robert H. Mitchell	07 22 1894	164	Seabright, N.J.
Sch Maria Louisa	10 10 1894	43	Spermaceti Cove, N.J.
Stmr Jamella	10 10 1894	80	Long Island Sound
Sch Salmon Washburn	11 05 1894	89	Eaton's Neck, N.Y.
Sch F. Greenville Russell	11 22 1894	173	Sandy Hook, N.J.
Sch. Oriole	11 25 1894	250	Hither Plain, LI, N.Y.
Sch. Clara E. Simpson	12 04 1894	391	Long Island Sound, N.Y.
Sloop E.A.Willis	12 26 1894	33	Long Island Sound, N.Y.
Barge Seth Low	01 14 1895	406	Jones Beach, N.Y.
Bktn Beatrice	01 25 1895	288	Spermaceti Cove, N.J.
Sch. R.A. Fisher	01 26 1895	971	Off Long Beach, N.J.
Brig Gem	02 06 1895	189	Moriches, LI, N.Y.
Sch. Louis V. Place	02 08 1895	735	Lone Hill, LI, N.Y.
Sch Marion F. Sprague	02 10 1895	787	Five Fathom Bank, N.J.
Stmr F.W. Vosburgh	03 12 1895	94	Romer Shoals, N.Y.
Stmr Olinda	06 11 1895		Fishers Island, N.Y.
Sch John Lenthall	07 25 1895	144	Fire Island, N.Y.
Stmr James W. Boyle	11 13 1895	41	Rockaway Inlet, N.Y.
Sch Cornelia M. Kingsland	11 23 1895	39	Sandy Hook, N.J.
Sloop Nile	03 04 1896	293	Long Island Sound, N.Y.
Sch Kate Scranton	03 11 1896	125	Eaton's Neck, N.Y.

NAME	DATE	TONS	LOCATION
Bark H.J. Libby	03 20 1896	621	Jones Beach, LI, N.Y.
Barge Imperial	04 01 1896	172	Cedar Creek, N.J.
Barge #8, CRR of N.J.	07 04 1896	686	Shinnecock, LI, N.Y.
Sch. Freestone	12 10 1896	71	Long Island Sound
Sch Grace K. Green	12 15 1896	406	Long Branch, N.J.
Sch Nahum Chapin	01 21 1897	597	Quogue, LI, N.Y.
Sch. Emily E. Johnson	03 24 1897	122	Monmouth Beach, N.J.
Sch. E.F.C. Young	05 01 1897	113	Spermaceti Cove, N.J.
Sch L.B. Gilchrist	05 04 1897	1,158	Amagansett, LI, N.Y.
Stmr Catskill	09 15 1897	816	No. River, N.Y.,Collision
Sch Richmond	10 20 1897	100	Squan Beach, N.J.
Tug William Howe	10 23 1897	33	New York Harbor.
Sch. Henry Finch	11 28 1897	1,976	Harvey Cedars, N.J.
Sch John Johnson	02 20 1898	315	Ship Bottom, N.J.
Stmr Delaware	07 08 1898	1,646	Forked River, N.J.
Sch Cinderella	11 12 1898	57	Fire Island Inlet, N.Y.
Sch. William M. Everett	11 18 1898	167	Shelter Island, N.Y.
Tug Governor	12 10 1898	84	Rockaway Point, N.Y.
Sch. Robert A. Snow	02 08 1899	174	Rockaway Point, N.Y.
Brt. Bktn. Brazil	02 10 1899	359	Moriches, LI, N.Y.
Sch. Bg. David Crockett	02 14 1899	1,506	New York harbor.
Sch May McFarland	02 27 1899	480	Point Lookout, LI, N.Y.
Sch Homer D. Alverson	03 07 1899	760	Lone Hill, LI, N.Y.
Sch. Ellangowan	04 08 1899	841	Near Montauk Point, N.Y.
Sch Mary and Eva	05 02 1899	58	Off Barnegat Light, N.J.
Sch John A McKie	07 16 1899	223	Ship Bottom, N.J.
Sch Romana	10 13 1899	26	Jones Beach, N.Y.
Stmr Nutmeg State	10 14 1899	1,024	Burned, L.I. Sound.
Ferry Chicago	10 31 1899	1,006	New York Harbor.
Can. Brig Plover	11 04 1899	405	Sandy Point, N.Y.
Sch Rabboni	12 30 1899	294	Rocky Point, N.Y.
Ship Josephus	05 07 1900	1,470	Constable Hook, N.J.
Sch John W. Fox	06 29 1900	82	Shark River, N.J.
Barge Texas	06 30 1900	149	Burned, Hoboken, N.J.
SS Bremen	06 30 1900		Hoboken, N.J.
SS Main	06 30 1900		Hoboken, N.J.
SS Saale	06 30 1900		Hoboken, N.J.
Sch Samuel Ricker	04 23 1901	64	Long Island Sound.
Sch A.R. Keene	05 10 1901	364	Point Lookout, N.Y.
Sch Lydia A. Harvey	05 13 1901	52	Romer Shoals, N.Y.
Italian Bark Bianca	05 23 1901	466	Ship Bottom, N.J.
Ferry Northfield	06 14 1901	600	New York Harbor.
Stmr Alert	07 04 1901	69	Barneget, N.J.
Ship Comm. T. H. Allen	07 19 1901	2,390	N.Y. harbor.
Sch James Gordon Bennett	08 17 1901	74	Sandy Hook, N.J.
Sch Lucy W. Snow	09 11 1901	315	Moriches, LI, N.Y.
Ferry Elizabeth	10 22 1901		New York harbor.
Stmr Robert Haddon	11 23 1901	87	Long Branch, N.J.
Sch. Barge Grant	11 24 1901	835	Chadwick, N.J.
Barge Wilmore	11 24 1901	844	Chadwick, N.J.
Sch. Barge Davis	11 24 1901	853	Squan Beach, N.J.
Sch Mark Gray	12 14 1901	308	Toms River, N.J.
Bark Sindia	12 15 1901		Ocean City, N.J.
Sch Bg Lichtenfels Bros	01 21 1902	1,136	New York Harbor.
Sch. Belle of Oregon	02 02 1902	1,115	Fire Island, N.Y.
Sch. Antelope	02 02 1902	1,306	Fire Island, N.Y.
Sch Brg John F. Randall	02 03 1902	1,643	Fire Island, N.Y.
Barge P.J. Carleton	03 05 1902		Sandy Hook, N.J.
Barge Ringleader	03 05 1902		Sandy Hook, N.J.
Stmr John Anson	04 24 1902	23	New York Harbor.

NAME	DATE	TONS	LOCATION
Sch Cornelia Soule	04 26 1902	306	Rockaway Point, N.Y.
Stmr Jacob Kuper	08 13 1902	144	New York Harbor.
Bark Alice Reed	12 03 1902	873	Napeague, N.Y.
Sp Shp Remedios-Pascual	01 03 1903	1,605	Ship Bottom, N.J.
Bktn Abiel Abbott	01 20 1903	589	Ship Bottom, N.J.
Barge Afton	05 01 1903	242	Long Island Sound.
Sch Fred A. Emerson	06 12 1903	122	Long Island Sound.
Ital Bk. Angela E. Maria	07 30 1903		Constable Hook, N.J.
Sch John Booth	08 26 1903	414	Long Island Sound.
Stmr. Saugerties	11 22 1903	848	Burned at Saugerties, NY
Can Bktn Cuba	12 18 1903	481	Ditch Plain, N.Y.
Sch G.M. Brainerd	01 12 1904	242	Long Island Sound.
Sch Augustus Hunt	01 22 1904	1,200	Quogue, LI, N.Y.
Stmr Tremont	02 08 1904	1,427	New York Harbor.
Sch Olive T. Whittier	02 22 1904	562	Ship Bottom, N.J.
Sch Benjamin C. Cromwell	02 22 1904	616	Fire Island Beach, N.Y.
Stmr General Slocum	06 15 1904	1,284	East River, NY.
Sch Glide	10 06 1904	54	Fire Island, N.Y.
Sch Wilson and Hunting	11 09 1904	418	Barnegat, N.J.
Barge C.T. No. 5	11 13 1904	177	Long Island Sound
Barge Kelsey	11 28 1904	203	New York, N.Y.
Stmr Glen Island	12 16 1904	614	Long Island Sound.
Sch Lizzie H. Brayton	12 18 1904	1,126	Bay Head, N.J.
Sch Frank W. McCullough	12 23 1904	127	Oak Island, LI, N.Y.
Br. Stmr. Drumelzier	12 26 1904	3,625	Fire Island, LI, N.Y.
Barge Samuel D. Carleton	01 25 1905	850	Off Sea Grit, N.J.
Steamer Clarence	01 25 1905	117	New York Harbor.
Barge Atlas	02 04 1905	423	Long Island City, N.Y.
Stmr. Seaconnet	05 29 1905	188	Shinnecock, LI, N.Y.
Stmr. Eclipse	05 29 1905	32	Fire Island, N.Y.
Stmr Hopatcong	08 07 1905	854	Hoboken, N.J.
mv Delta	08 07 1905	19	Burned, East River, N.Y.
Bg. William H. Vanderbilt	08 19 1905	241	New York, N.Y.
Barge John Neilson	08 19 1905	344	New York, N.Y.
Sch. Marion E. Rockhill	08 21 1905	284	Amagansett, LI, N.Y.
Barge Abram Collerd	09 11 1905	217	New York, N.Y.
Barge Star	09 12 1905	89	New York, N.Y.
Stmr Bridgeport	09 28 1905	125	Off Yonkers, N.Y.
Stmr John McCausland	10 11 1905	33	Turkey Point, N.Y.
Sch Custis W. Wright	10 15 1905	113	Barnegat, N.J.
Stmr Nautilus (Burned)	10 19 1905	24	Fishers Island, N.Y.
Stmr James D. Leary	10 25 1905	76	Newark Bay, N.J.
Stmr Alert	12 16 1905	170	Hell Gate, N.Y.
Stmr. Ariosa	01 04 1906	140	Romer Shoals, N.Y.
Sch Stephen Woolsey	01 24 1906	32	Montauk Point, N.Y.
Barge Dom Pedro	02 21 1906	193	New York, N.Y.
Barge Myndert Starin	03 03 1906	203	Weehawken, N.J.
Barge Hamilton Fish	03 06 1906	1,616	Off Barnegat, N.J.
Sch Martha E. McCabe	03 20 1906	345	Barnegat, N.J.
Bg. Jen. & Flornc. Cahill	03 22 1906	168	Oyster Bay, N.Y.
Sch Nettie Cushing	04 16 1906	111	Rocky Point, LI, N.Y.
Stmr City of Detroit	04 18 1906	118	St. George, N.Y.
Sch. E.C. Hay	06 28 1906	63	New York City.
Sch. Vinland	07 04 1906	965	Off Rikers Island, N.Y.
Barge Kingston	07 04 1906	1,070	Off Shinnecock, LI, N.Y.
Sch Eglet	07 10 1906	130	North River, N.Y.
Stmr Ella Powell	10 11 1906	133	Long Island Sound.
Barge M.P.Grace	11 13 1906	1,934	Shinnecock, N.Y.
Sch James M. Hall	11 15 1906	87	Long Branch, N.J.
Stmr J.D.Scott	11 22 1906	87	Off Pultneyville, N.Y.

NAME	DATE	TONS	LOCATION
Barge Buena Ventura	12 07 1906	1,660	Off Montauk Point, N.Y.
Sch Hermit	12 15 1906	70	Off Sandy Hook, N.J.
Stmr Paterson	12 29 1906	1,057	North River, N.Y.
Sch. Blanche Morgan	01 09 1907	44	Brooklyn, N.Y.
Barge Honesdale	01 10 1907	277	Fishers Island, N.Y.
Barge Delaware	01 10 1907	294	Fishers Island, N.Y.
Bark Charles Loring	02 02 1907	552	Off Sandy Hook, N.J.
Sch Helen J. Seitz	02 09 1907	2,547	Long Beach, N.J.
Stmr City of Troy	04 05 1907	1,527	Dobbs Ferry, N.Y.
Sch. William D. Becker	04 07 1907	1,046	Off Barnegat, N.J.
Barge Susquehanna	04 22 1907	314	Long Island Sound
Barge Kenneth W. McNeil	05 07 1907	261	New York, N.Y.
Stmr Anna J. Kipp	05 08 1907	42	New York, N.Y.
Barge Wm. T. Howes	05 14 1907	600	Long Island Sound.
Bg.Lydia B. Cowperthwaite	05 29 1907	271	Long Island Sound, N.Y.
Sch Emily and Irene	06 01 1907	33	Great Peconic Bay, N.Y.
Sch T. Charlton Henry	06 23 1907	2,241	Fire Island, N.Y.
Sch Myronus	08 12 1907	283	Long Island Sound.
Schooner Julia	09 13 1907	57	Coney Island, N.Y.
Barge Castleton	10 01 1907	412	New York, N.Y.
Barge Teutonic	10 08 1907	253	Long Island Sound
Sch Carrie C. Miles	10 15 1907	106	Dry Romer Shoal, N.Y.
Sch. Annie Sargent	10 16 1907	66	Bayville Creek, LI, N.Y.
Sch William Voorhis	11 02 1907	89	New York, N.Y.
Sch. Crystall	11 15 1907	28	Kill Van Kull, N.Y.
Sch. Phoebe Ann	11 17 1907	32	East River, N.Y.
Sch. Bg. Number 26	11 27 1907	1,566	Barnegat, N.J.
Bark Edmund Phinney	12 14 1907	751	Sandy Hook, N.J.
Barge Addie Jordon	12 14 1907	376	Squan Beach, N.J.
Barge Ellis P. Rogers	12 23 1907	68	New York, N.Y.
Sch. Estelle Phinney	12 27 1907	922	Barnegat, N.J.
Sch. Julia Davis	01 02 1908	58	Fishers Island, N.Y.
Barge Helen	01 07 1908	388	Fishers Island, N.Y.
Sch. Bge. Gwennie	01 24 1908	1,087	25 Mi-NE-Barnegat, N.J.
Barge Fannie	01 24 1908	948	Barnegat, N.J.
Sch. Bg. Matanzas	01 27 1908	1,579	Montauk, LI, N.Y.
Barge Addie B. Bacon	02 10 1908	422	Flynns Knoll, N.Y. Bay.
Sch Howard B. Peck	02 15 1908	472	Fire Island, N.Y.
Sch. Deborah T. Hill	03 31 1908	37	East River, N.Y.
Barge William H. Wessels	04 28 1908	277	Sands Point, LI, N.Y.
Ger. Ship Peter Rickmers	04 30 1908	2,958	Short Beach, LI, N.Y.
Barge David E. Baxter	05 08 1908	173	St. Geroge, Staten Isl,NY
Sch Jordan Wooley	05 31 1908	37	Long Island Sound, N.Y.
Slp. Bg. Buffalo	07 18 1908	482	Fishers Island Sound N.Y.
Sloop Ariel	09 21 1908	54	Burned at New York, N.Y.
Stmr New York	10 20 1908	1,974	Burned, Newburgh, N.Y.
Sch. Jeannie Thomas	11 16 1908	691	300 Mi E.-Sandy Hook, NJ.
Stmr. Finance	11 26 1908	2,603	New York Bay
Barge Number 22	01 17 1909	936	Barnegat, N.J.
Br. Sch. Swallow	01 17 1909	73	Long Island Sound.
Sch. Bg. John A. Briggs	01 20 1909	2,086	Barnegat, N.J.
Br. Stmr Republic	01 23 1909		Sunk Ambrose Shipway
Sch Miles M. Merry	02 17 1909	1,589	Moriches, LI, N.Y.
Sch William H. Conner	03 22 1909	1,514	Sandy Hook, N.J.
Sch. Bg. Samar	03 25 1909	1,082	Highlands, N.J.
Sch Bg. Wm. H. Conner	04 22 1909	1,514	Sandy Hook, N.J.
Sch William C. Carnegie	05 01 1909	2,663	Moriches, LI, N.Y.
Barge Berkshire	05 23 1909	1,192	Off Sandy Hook, N.J.
Sch. Perkasie	07 08 1909	956	Off Barnegat, N.J.
Stmr Martha Stevens	07 20 1909	283	New York Harbor.

NAME	DATE	TONS	LOCATION
Stmr Kenosha	07 24 1909	1,697	Fire Island, N.Y.
Sch Arlington	08 17 1909	592	Long Beach, LI, N.Y.
Sch. Shawmont	08 17 1909	954	Off Shinnecock, LI, N.Y.
Barge Helen R.	10 05 1909	284	Flushing, N.Y.
Sch. Henry Wardell	12 20 1909	69	Perth Amboy, N.J.
Sch Superior	12 25 1909	46	Sea Cliff, N.Y.
Stmr Thurmond	12 26 1909	1,252	Toms River, N.J.
Sch. John A. Briggs	12 26 1909	2,965	Near Barnegat, N.J.
Stmr Olin J. Stephens	12 31 1909	34	Mattituck, N.Y.
It. Bk. Fortuna	01 18 1910	924	Ship Bottom, N.J.
J. Henry Edmunds	02 01 1910	284	Sandy Hook, N.J.
Sch. Franklin D. Nelson	02 11 1910	29	Sandy Hook, N.J.
Stmr John T. Pratt	03 25 1910	60	Glen Cove, N.Y.
Tug Reliable (Burned)	04 19 1910	49	New Rochelle, N.Y.
Stmr Poughkeepsie	06 26 1910	810	Highland, N.Y.
Sloop Ceres (Burned)	07 16 1910	47	New York, N.Y.
Stmr William Orr	09 07 1910	31	Coney Island Creek, N.Y.
Sch Emily Baxter	11 26 1910	53	Fire Island Inlet, N.Y.
Stmr Peekskill	12 12 1910	190	Verplanck Point, N.Y.
Barge Port Royal	12 14 1910	298	Hell Gate, N.Y.
Barge Frank Miller	12 14 1910	274	Hell Gate, N.Y.
Stmr Howard	03 06 1911	179	Jones Beach, LI, N.Y.
Sch Robert T. Graham	07 14 1911	70	Fire Island, N.Y.
Stmr Henry H. Stanwood	08 12 1911	44	New York, N.Y.
Sch. Josie R. Burt	08 30 1911	760	Barnegat, N.J.
Sch Oliver Mitchell	09 26 1911	320	Long Island Sound.
Barge Searsport	11 12 1911	1,159	1 Mi S, Fire Island, N.Y.
Sch. Bg. Helen A. Wyman	11 19 1911	1,717	Montauk Point, LI, N.Y.
Stmr Jose	03 13 1912		Jamaica, N.Y.
Sch Bg. Thaxter	03 15 1912	843	12 Mi SE of Shinnecock NY
Stmr Precurser	06 14 1912	57	Port Jefferson, N.Y.
Stmr Idler	07 24 1912	57	New York, N.Y.
Ship Concordia	10 10 1912		Constable Hook, N.J.
Stmr Dunholme	10 10 1912		Constable Hook, N.J.
Sch. Copy	10 15 1912	86	Eatons Neck, LI, N.Y.
Ital. Bk. Caterina	10 23 1912	1,350	Forked River, N.J.
Sch DeMory Gray	11 08 1912	401	Long Island, N.Y.
Bg.Maryland,Ex Gen Slocum	12 04 1912	625	Sank, Ludlum Beach, N.J.
Sch L. Herbert Taft	12 19 1912	1,492	Sandy Hook, N.J.
Sch John H. May	12 24 1912	363	Sandy Hook, N.J.
Stmr Margaret	12 30 1912	203	Near Avalon, N.J.
Barge Anna R	02 05 1913	405	Long Island, N.Y.
Barge Violet Blossom	02 20 1913	374	New York, N.Y.
Barge Richard Jackson	03 06 1913	230	New York, N.Y.
Stmr Fordham(Burned)	04 07 1913	728	Shooter Island, N.Y.
Sch Bg. Wayne	04 16 1913	820	Sank off Barnegat, N.J.
Sch. Bg. Ardmore	04 16 1913	821	Barnegat, N.J.
Sch. Burnside	04 20 1913	855	Off Fire Island Ltshp,NY
Stmr Robert Rogers	10 11 1913	142	New York, N.Y.
Sch. Charles Atkinson	10 13 1913	68	Mattinicock Point, LI, NY
Sch Marjory Brown	10 20 1913	1,210	Off Long Island, N.Y.
Stmr Charles E. Soper	10 30 1913	42	Off Larchmont, N.Y.
Sch. A.J. Miller	11 09 1913	110	Long Island Sound, N.Y.
Stmr Buffalo	11 21 1913	131	Staten Island, N.Y.
Sch. Bg. Undaunted	12 26 1913	1,768	Forked River, N.J.
Sch Bg. A.G. Ropes	12 26 1913	2,438	Forked River, N.J.
Stmr Ice King	12 28 1913	138	Off Sandy Hook, N.Y.
Stmr Oklahoma	01 04 1914	5,583	Off Sandy Hook, N.J.
Barge Baravia	01 23 1914	1,227	Montauk Point, LI, N.Y.
Barge Maggie Feeney	02 14 1914	333	Rocky Point, N.Y.

NAME	DATE	TONS	LOCATION
Barge Rose Marie Feeney	02 14 1914	461	Long Island Sound.
Barge Katie Woods	02 14 1914	358	Long Island Sound.
Sch. Bg. Felix	03 01 1914	1,174	Off Fire Island, N.Y.
Stmr Charlemagne Tower Jr	03 06 1914	1,825	Cedar Creek, N.J.
Barge Evening Star	04 12 1914	250	Off Hell Gate, N.Y.
Sch Charles K. Buckley	04 15 1914	507	Off Long Branch, N.J.
Barge B.W. O'Hara	05 11 1914	227	New York Harbor, N.Y.
Stmr New Jersey	07 10 1914	478	Off Sandy Hook, N.Y.
Stmr Matchless	07 20 1914	163	Arthur Kills, N.Y.
Stmr L. Boyer	09 23 1914	197	Jamaica Bay, N.Y.
Bg. Ludlow (Burned)	11 03 1914	413	Pier 22, Brooklyn, N.Y.
Sch Charles Lawrence	11 09 1914	436	Long Island Sound.
Barge Roderick C. McNeil	11 19 1914	214	Long Island Sound, N.Y.
Barge Carlos French	12 20 1914	433	Long Island Sound.
Barge Mathilde R	01 05 1915	219	Hell Gate, N.Y.
Sch. Bg. R.R. Thomas	01 07 1915	1,393	Off Shinnecock Lt. LI,NY.
mv Manhassett	03 25 1915	112	East End, L.I., N.Y.
Barge Slp. Parks	05 07 1915	474	Eatons Neck, LI, N.Y.
Sch. M.V.B. Chase	08 04 1915	457	Sandy Hook, N.J.
Stmr Isabel	09 28 1915	421	Long Island Sound.
Sch. Bg. Knickerbocker	10 19 1915	2,381	Barnegat Inlet, N.Y.
Sch. Bg. Knickerbocker	11 04 1915	954	Off Montauk Point, N.Y.
Barge Minnie D. Kennelly	02 04 1916	371	Long Island Sound.
Ship John Bossert	02 15 1916	601	New York, NY.
Ship Jacob A. Stamler	02 17 1916	1,198	New York, N.Y.
Barge Arundel	04 09 1916	418	Barnegat, N.J.
Barge Harry R. Conners	05 25 1916	230	Harlem River, N.Y.
Stmr Keyport	07 22 1916		Battery, N.Y.
Sch George E. Walcott	07 30 1916	1,553	Black Tom, N.J.
mv Emma E. Overton	08 19 1916	35	Off Long Island, N.Y.
Barge John S. Thompson	11 23 1916	239	Long Island Sound, N.Y.
Sch. Bg. 792	11 24 1916	532	Long Island Sound, N.Y.
Barge Edward Olney, Jr	11 25 1916	337	Long Island Sound, N.Y.
Barge Frank P. Scully	12 06 1916	303	Falkners Island, N.Y.
U.S.S. Sumner	12 11 1916		Barnegat, N.J.
Sch. Bg. Kennebec	02 05 1917	2,048	Off Sandy Hook, N.J.
Barge Thomas Hale	02 05 1917	207	Brooklyn, N.Y.
Sch. Bg. Iowa	02 05 1917	1,606	Off Sandy Hook, N.J.
Sch. Bg. Frank Pendleton	03 08 1917	1,393	Ambrose Channel, N.Y.
Sch. Bg. Henry Clay	04 06 1917	841	Off Montauk Point, N.Y.
mv Evelyn (Burned)	04 12 1917	69	Bay Shore, N.Y.
Sch Sallie E. Ludlam	06 17 1917	237	New York Harbor.
Sch Florence	06 25 1917	75	Off Eatons Neck, LI, N.Y.
Sch. Bg. Number 782	08 10 1917	924	Off Shinnecock Lt. LI, NY
Sch. J.A. Holmes	09 08 1917	167	Off Barnegat, N.J.
Sch. Bg. Foster	09 08 1917	841	Off New Jersey
Stmr Broadway	09 19 1917	755	New York, N.Y.
Barge Cassie	10 24 1917	948	Sandy Hook, N.J.
Stmr. James Logan	11 17 1917	201	New York, N.Y.
Barge S.E.Vincent	01 02 1918	290	Off Throggs Pt. N.Y.
Barge Blue Point	01 18 1918	300	Whitestone, L.I., N.Y.
Sch. Bg. Somerset	02 10 1918	629	Off Ambrose Light, N.Y.
Barge Belle F. Messick	02 26 1918	350	Brooklyn, N.Y.
Barge Annie Bulger	02 26 1918	233	New York Harbor.
Barge Baby Blue	04 06 1918	463	New York, N.Y.
Barge Cullen # 180	04 17 1918	424	East River, N.Y.
Sch. Jacob Haskell	05 31 1918	1,778	Off Barnegat, N.J.
Sch Edward H. Cole	05 31 1918	1,791	Off Barnegat, N.J.
SS San Diego	07 19 1918		Off Long Island, N.Y.
Stmr Frederick R. Kellog	08 13 1918		Ambrose Channel, N.Y.

NAME	DATE	TONS	LOCATION
Sch Dorothy B. Barrett	08 14 1918	2,088	5 Fathom Bank, N.J.
Stmr Roudolph	09 25 1918	200	New York, N.Y.
Stmr San Saba	10 04 1918	2,458	SE-Barnegat, N.J.
Sch Bg. J.H.Rutter	10 23 1918	1,224	Off Pier 20, No River,NY.
Stmr Queens	11 09 1918	802	New York, N.Y.
Stmr Armitage E. Brearly	12 05 1918	237	Stone Harbor, N.J.
Nor. SS Nils	12 17 1918		West Banks, N.Y. (sunk)
Stmr Lord Dufferin	02 28 1919		N.Y. harbor, collision.
Tug William A. Jamison	05 17 1919	229	New York harbor.
Stmr W.L. Webster	06 03 1919	73	Brooklyn, N.Y.
Sch. Charles E. Dunlap	07 22 1919	1,609	Far Rockaway Beach, N.J.
Barge Red Lion	08 15 1919	455	East River, N.Y.
Stmr Point Comfort	09 17 1919	629	Esopus Island, N.Y.
mv Priscilla	09 19 1919	44	Rockaway Shoals, N.Y.
mv Geneva Mertis	10 15 1919	50	Rockaway Inlet, N.Y.
Barge Dorothy	11 14 1919	393	Plum Island, N.Y.
Barge Nellie T.	11 14 1919	255	Brooklyn, N.Y.
Stmr Ashford	11 ?? 1919	132	Schenectady, N.Y.
Sch Mary E. Lynch	12 05 1919	185	North River, N.Y.
Barge Louis H. St. John	12 09 1919		New York harbor.
Stmr St. Louis	01 08 1920	10230	Hoboken, N.J.
Stmr Kaskaskia	01 31 1920	2,934	New York, N.Y.
Stmr Maine	02 04 1920	2,395	Execution Rocks, N.Y.
Barge Yankee	02 04 1920	531	Brooklyn, N.Y.
Stmr Princess Anne	02 06 1920	3,629	Rockaway Shoals, N.Y.
Stmr Queensboro	02 15 1920	254	New York, N.Y.
Barge Bernard F. Guinan	02 18 1920	322	Yonkers, N.Y.
Stmr Rosailie	03 07 1920	209	Hudson River, N.Y.
Stmr William V.R. Smith	03 11 1920	207	New York, N.Y.
Sch Bg. No. 10	03 14 1920	897	Off Montauk Point, N.Y.
Stmr Hallfried(Burned)	04 20 1920		Bush Terminal, Brooklyn
mv Norma	04 28 1920	111	Near Point Lookout, N.Y.
Stmr William O'Brien	04 ?? 1920	5,211	Left N.Y., Lost at Sea.
Sch Florence Thurlow	05 12 1920	1,042	Sea Girt, N.J.
Stmr Coastwise	07 19 1920	208	Near Fire Island, N.Y.
Stmr Snug Harbor	08 15 1920	2,388	Long Island, N.Y.
Sch Bg. Vermilion	09 14 1920	1,208	Montauk Point Light, N.Y.
Sch. Bg. John H. Winstead	09 14 1920	841	Montauk Pt. Light, N.Y.
Sch Benjamin E. Weeks	11 01 1920	77	New York, N.Y.
Stmr Chrystenah	11 16 1920	571	New Rochelle, N.Y.
Stmr Ticeline	11 22 1920	99	New York, N.Y.
Barge Mgt. Julia Howard	11 27 1920	502	New York, N.Y.
Stmr John V. Craven	12 29 1920	183	New York, N.Y.
Sch Amos Briggs	04 14 1921	93	Off Sandy Hook, N.J.
Ship Granite State	05 23 1921		New York harbor.
Stmr Kennebec	06 18 1921	2,183	Near Barnegat Light, N.J.
Stmr Marion	08 10 1921	39	East River, N.Y.
Barge Caddo	08 26 1921	432	Off Barnegat, N.J.
Stmr Malden	09 17 1921	5,054	Montuak, L.I., N.Y.
Stmr Antionette	10 14 1921	221	Jamaica Bay, N.Y.
Sch. Bg. Governor Robie	11 28 1921	1,712	Off Highlands Light, N.J.
Sch Thomas R. Woolley	11 28 1921	104	Montauk Point, N.Y.
Sch Bg. Helen	01 12 1922	1,285	Off Sea Girt, N.J.
Sch Bg. Grace	01 12 1922	877	Off Sea Girt, N.J.
Sch Bessie A. White	02 06 1922		Long Island, N.Y.
Sch Orlando V. Wooten	04 07 1922	677	Barnegat, N.J.
Stmr Eagle Boat # 17	05 19 1922		Amagansett, LI, N.Y.
Sch Bg. Cienfuegos	05 27 1922	1,915	Off Barnegat, N.J.
Stmr Charnley	07 15 1922	83	Port Jefferson Harbor NY.
Barge John T. Hughes	08 08 1922	490	Hell Gate, N.Y.

NAME	DATE	TONS	LOCATION
Stmr Mohawk	08 09 1922	1,414	Kill Van Kull, N.Y.
Stmr Dorothea	08 12 1922	96	Montauk, L.I., N.Y.
Stmr H.C. Rowe & Co.	10 31 1922	500	Long Island, N.Y.
Sch Bg. Number Seventeen	11 16 1922	935	New York Harbor.
Sch. Bg. Albany	11 16 1922	659	New York Harbor.
Barges Albany & # 17	11 16 1922		New York Harbor.
Stmr Phillip J. Kenny	01 19 1923	142	Ambrose Channel, N.Y.
Barge Sara A. Johnson	04 05 1923	412	New York Harbor.
Sch Bg. Wellesley	04 16 1923	1,306	Off New Jersey.
Barge Frank Jenkins	05 28 1923	375	Hell Gate, N.Y.
Stmr Essex	06 05 1923	389	Beach Haven, N.J.
Stmr Cornelia	06 25 1923	38	Pier 2, N. River, N.Y.
Stmr Halcyon	10 18 1923	89	Coney Island, N.Y.
Sch Charlie & Willie	10 30 1923	123	New York, N.Y.
Stmr Henry Rowe	11 17 1923	220	North River, N.Y.
Barge Northern # 8	01 16 1924	673	Off Long Branch, N.J.
Stmr Squantum	01 16 1924	248	Brooklyn, N.Y.
Barge Norman	01 31 1924	372	Off Gov. Isl, N.Y.
Stmr Ivanhoe	02 17 1924	119	Kill Van Kull, N.Y.
Bgtn U.S. # 110(Concrete)	03 07 1924	204	Brooklyn, N.Y.
Barge Plymouth	03 31 1924	474	Long Branch, N.J.
Stmr Charlie McAlister	04 21 1924	136	Brooklyn, N.Y.
Stmr Highlander	04 26 1924	1,310	W 155th St, New York, NY.
Stmr. Grand Republic	04 26 1924	1,760	W 155th St, New York, NY.
SS C.A.M. Church	04 26 1924		W 155th St, New York, NY.
Lighter Nassau	04 26 1924	300	W 155th St, New York, NY.
Bark Benmore	07 10 1924	1,478	New York, N.Y.
Stmr Mistletoe	10 05 1924	362	Sandy Hook, N.J.
mv Nomad	11 16 1924	78	Old Field Pt. LI, N.Y.
Sch Commmack	01 20 1925	1,446	Sandy Hook, N.J.
Stmr Visitor	04 20 1925	70	Flushing, LI, N.Y.
Stmr Traffic	04 30 1925	203	City Island, N.Y.
Sch Bg. Shamokin	05 11 1925	829	Scotland Ltshp, N.Y.
Stmr Corvalis	06 16 1925	2,922	Sandy Hook, N.J.
Sch Malvern	09 07 1925	8434	Montauk Point, N.Y.
Stmr El Grudor	12 05 1925	103	Pelham Bay, N.Y.
Sch Bg. Ormond	01 09 1926	1,313	Highlands, N.J.
Sch Bg. T.J. Hooper	01 09 1926	722	Highlands, N.J.
Sch. Pheonix	02 03 1926	901	New York, N.Y.
Sch Bg. Number 20	02 04 1926	940	Barnegat, N.J.
Sch Bg. Searsport	02 04 1926	1,321	Off Barnegat, N.J.
Sch Bg. Number 21	02 04 1926	905	Barnegat, N.J.
Sch Bg. Number 28	02 04 1926	1,035	Barnegat, N.J.
Stmr N.Y. Marine Co #6	02 17 1926	179	Brooklyn, N.Y.
Brgtn Universe	04 02 1926	420	New York, N.Y.
Stmr Henry D. McCord	04 18 1926	69	Brooklyn, N.Y.
Stmr R.C. Reynolds	04 28 1926	409	Newburgh, N.Y.
Stmr Washington Irving	06 01 1926	3,104	New York, N.Y.
Stmr Panuco	06 02 1926	102	Brooklyn, N.Y.
Stmr Martin Kehoe	08 04 1926	111	Rockaway Inlet, N.Y.
Sch Bg. Bethayres	10 20 1926	955	Shinnecock Light, N.Y.
Stmr Edward T. Dalzell	10 26 1926	96	Brooklyn, N.Y.
Stmr Gen. Meigs	10 27 1926	267	New York, N.Y.
mv Alfred & Edwin	12 19 1926	109	Brooklyn, N.Y.
Stmr Wright	01 02 1927	96	Long Beach, N.Y.
Sch Leviathan	01 12 1927	109	East River, N.Y.
Stmr Cape Cod	02 05 1927	557	Astoria Ferry, N.Y.
Stmr El Sol	03 11 1927	6,008	New York, N.Y.
Bgtn Northern # 19	05 23 1927	739	Romer Shoals, N.Y.
Stmr Red Ash	07 07 1927	117	Staten Island, N.Y.

NAME	DATE	TONS	LOCATION
Slp Diver	10 13 1927	144	No. Rye Beach, N.Y.
Sch Bg. John H. Winstead	12 05 1927	1,160	Sea Girt Light, N.J.
Stmr Seneca	01 09 1928	2,963	New York, N.Y.
Sch Bg. Aransas	01 29 1928	1,312	Barnegat Light, N.J.
Sch Bg. Seneca	02 18 1928	2,208	Sandy Hook, N.J.
Stmr Keansburg	04 16 1928	498	Newburgh, N.Y.
Stmr Two Brothers	04 20 1928	139	Rockaway Point, LI, N.Y.
Bgtn Mary E. Joyce	06 13 1928	361	Yonkers, N.Y.
Sch Bg. Catonsville	06 29 1928	1,281	Barnegat Light, N.J.
Stmr Chancellor	07 31 1928	383	Staten Island, N.Y.
Stmr Fillet	10 03 1928	537	Montauk Point, N.Y.
Stmr James A. Cox	04 30 1928	61	Rockaway Beach, N.Y.
Bgtn Fairport	01 09 1929	212	Little Hell Gate, N.Y.
Bgtn. Raymond T. McNally	04 10 1929	457	Highlands, N.J.
Stmr Mathiasen Sisters	06 15 1929	167	Jones Inlet, L.I., N.Y.
Bgtn T.W. O. Company # 23	03 01 1930	312	Staten Island, N.Y.
Stmr Paragon	05 21 1930	142	Kill Van Kull, N.Y.
Stmr Evangeline	07 10 1930	314	Rockaway, LI, N.Y.
Sch Bg. Pocono	09 05 1930	698	Atlantic Highlands, N.J.
Stmr Roger C. Sullivan	03 05 1931	179	Long Island, N.Y.
Stmr Joyce Card	03 07 1931	123	Brooklyn, N.Y.
mv Trimount	05 07 1931	124	Long Island Sound, N.Y.
Stmr Marion Olsen	08 22 1931	87	Brooklyn, N.Y.
Bgtn Cecelia Dunlap	09 12 1931	835	Scotland Lightship, N.Y.
Stmr City of Stamford	10 27 1931	427	East River, N.Y.
Stmr Sea Bird(Burned)	05 09 1932	489	152 St, E. River, N.Y.
Stmr Albertine (Burned)	05 09 1932	558	East River, N.Y.
Stmr New York	07 18 1932	770	Staten Island, N.Y.
Stmr Observation	09 07 1932	122	East River, N.Y.
Stmr Transport	03 22 1933	162	Brooklyn, N.Y.
Bgtn. Number Eighteen	04 22 1933	936	East River, N.Y.
Bgtn Ramos	06 30 1933	1,208	Scotland Lightship, N.Y.
Bgtn. Rob Roy	10 05 1933	466	Barnegat, N.J.
Stmr J.P. McAlister	05 18 1934	133	Brooklyn, N.Y.
Bgtn. Truro	05 26 1934	1,631	No. Barnegat Ltshp. N.J.
Sch Bg. Irene	05 26 1934	1,208	Off Barnegat Light, N.J.
Bgtn William S. Keeler	07 10 1934	476	Execution Rocks LI, N.Y.
mv Annie L. Wilcox	07 26 1934	158	Long Island Sound.
Liner Morro Castle	09 08 1934	11520	Sea Girt, N.J.
Bgtn Maud L. Foster	10 27 1934	423	Hudson River, N.Y.
Stmr Lexington	01 02 1935	1,248	East River, N.Y.
Bgtn. Coast Trans Co #2	01 06 1935	263	Astoria, LI, N.Y.
Stmr Mohawk	01 25 1935	5,896	Sea Girt, N.J.
Stmr Alice	01 28 1935	154	Erie Basin, Brooklyn, NY.
Bgtn. Reardon Bros	05 19 1935	236	Hudson River, N.Y.
Bgtn Seth H. Linthicum	06 19 1935	1,026	Off Barnegat Light, N.J.
Stmr Helen M Mathiasen	06 22 1935	137	Pier 21, Brooklyn, N.Y.
Stmr John G. Olsen	08 04 1935	134	Pier 21, Brooklyn, N.Y.
Stmr. Secausus	11 03 1935	919	Brooklyn, N.Y.
Bgtn Brooklyn	05 29 1936	1,880	Kill Van Kull, S.I., N.Y.

The New York Maritime Register.

Circulates in Every Part of the World.
ESTABLISHED 1869.

Volume 54. No. 30.— Whole Number 2904.
Subscription $35 per annum. No single copies for sale.

NEW YORK, WEDNESDAY, JULY 25, 1923.
PUBLISHED WEEKLY BY THE WORLD'S MARITIME NEWS CO., AT NOS 88 & 90 GOLD STREET.

Entered as Second Class Matter June 20, 1879, at the Post
Office at New York, N. Y., under the Act of March 3, 1879.